THINGS OF CHINA
Catholic missionary attempts in XVI century China

SERGIO TICOZZI

THINGS OF CHINA

Catholic missionary attempts in XVI century China

CHORABOOKS
HONG KONG 2024

Immagine di copertina di Aurelio Porfiri. Tutti i diritti riservati.

INDICE

INTRODUCTION
Aurelio Porfiri

The topic of the relationship between China and the Catholic Church is fascinating and also a source of many concerns. The cultural diversity inherent in our being "social animals" often leads to worldviews that are almost irreconcilably in contrast. You may ask, why would a musician like me be concerned with China? Because I have lived in China for more than 8 years, I have taught in Macao and Shanghai, and I have had extensive experience in Hong Kong as well. For more than 20 years, I have been interested in the Chinese world, studying its culture, language, music, and painting. Therefore, I believe I have some minimal credentials to say something about the text you are about to read.

It is a text by Father Sergio Ticozzi, a missionary of PIME who has lived in Hong Kong for more than 50 years and who has already authored important works aimed at understanding the difficult relationship between the Celestial Empire and the Catholic Church. As I mentioned, the topic of the relationship between China and the Catholic Church is so fascinating that it has filled libraries with books in all languages. What does this relationship ultimately boil down to? To the Catholic Church's desire to evangelize China. Many attempts have been made for this evangelization to "inculturate" (as it is said today) the Christian message for the Chinese. These attempts have not always been successful and have often yielded very little in terms of results. Christianity has been present in China since at least the 7th century, through the preaching of the Syriac Church or Church of the East (improperly called the "Nestorian Church"). This date is attested by the famous stele of Xi'an, though some trace it back to the very beginnings of Christianity. But we will stick here to what most scholars consider plausible. Among Catholic attempts, two must certainly be mentioned, one less known from the Franciscans in the 13th century and the much more famous one by the Jesuits starting in the 16th century, with the most representative figure being Matteo Ricci. Father Ticozzi's text deals specifically with the missionary efforts of the 16th century, a time certainly of great fervor. The Jesuits encountered the China of the Ming dynasty, which had replaced the Mongol Yuan dynasty, known to the Franciscans. The Ming dynasty ended in 1644, but the Christian presence did not, continuing even under the subsequent Qing dynasty, which remained in power until the end of the imperial era in 1911. Even after that time, Christianity continued to develop in China, facing great difficulties with the rise of communism led by Mao Zedong. The difficult relationship between Christianity and communism continues to this day, and the various initiatives put forth by the Holy See are subject to close scrutiny but also strong criticism.

And yet, the effort has always been to ensure that the Chinese people, with their great culture and rich history, could encounter the equally glorious history, culture, and spirituality of the Catholic Church. These missionary efforts have sought to foster this encounter so that the Chinese, too, could meet Christ, know Him, and love Him.

The text you are about to read by Father Sergio Ticozzi is not a narrative solely of triumphs and conquests, but also of failures and frustrations. Personally, I believe that the path of the Church in China has been one where progress was achieved through the immense sacrifice of missionaries and Chinese believers who wished to bring Christ to their fellow countrymen. This is also a story of martyrdom, a martyrdom that has accompanied the history of the Chinese Catholic Church until recent years. Some may call it an epic, and certainly, that term is not out of place. The Catholic religion has been in China for many centuries and is a reflection of Christ's Passion, with the hope that it will soon also be a reflection of His Resurrection.

CHRONOLOGY OF THE MAIN EVENTS

1319: The Portuguese Order of the Knights of Christ, which has accepted the ideological inheritance and properties after the suppression of the Templars in 1312, was recognized by Pope John XXII as the *Militia Jesu Christi* with the Bull *Ad ea ex quibus cultus*.

1368: In China, end of the Yuan (Mongol) Dynasty and beginning of the Ming Dynasty (until 1644). In 1381 and in 1394, the first Ming Emperor, Hongwu, forbad maritime trade to all civilians and cut off all travels with overseas countries (*haijin*, maritime band, 1397).

1385-1433: John I ruled as king of Portugal.

1402: Henry III of Castille started to colonize the Canary Islands.

1403-1424: Yongle Emperor in China.

1404: The maritime ban was cancelled to allow the seven travels of Zhenghe (Ma He, 1371-1433) from 1405 to 1433. But prohibitory decrees were again issued, causing people, especially of Zhejiang and Fujian, to turn to piracy.

1410: The Holy See joined the See of Khanbaliq with the See of Sultanieh, in Persia, under the Dominican archbishop John; however, bishops of Peking were still appointed up to the year 1475.

1415: Portuguese conquest of Ceuta (North Africa), followed by the discovery of Madeira Islands (1419) and the Azores (1427).

1417- 1431: Pope Martin V.

1420: Prince Henry (1394-1460, the Navigator) was appointed Prior/Master of the Order of the Knights of Christ.

1426-1435: Xuande Emperor in China.

1433: Eugene IV awarded all the islands, conquered and to be conquered to the Portuguese Order of the Knights of Christ.

1436-1449: Zhengtong Emperor in China.

1450-1456: Jingtai Emperor in China.

1454: The Bull *Romanus Pontifex* of Nicholas V (r. 1447-1455) affirmed the right of the Portuguese to the occupation of all 'pagan' lands, that might be discovered along the West coast of Africa.

1456: Pope Callixtus III (r. 1455-1458) gave to Prince Henry, the Prior of the Order of the Knights of Christ in Portugal, the spiritual administration over all the existing and future dominions of Portugal.

1457-1464: Tianshun Emperor in China.

1465-1487: Chenghua Emperor in China.

1474, September 4: Treaty of Alcaçovas settled the dispute between Portugal and Castille about the African islands.

1479: Birth of 'Spain' (España), under the rule of Ferdinand of Aragon and Isabel of Castille.

1487-1488: On behalf of Portugal, Bartholomew Diaz reached the Cape of Good Hope and Africa coasts.

1487-1505: Hongzhi Emperor in China.

1492-1503: Pope Alexander VI (1431-1503), who mainly with the Bull *Inter Coetera* (1493) entrusted with the *padroado* (patronage) the two Iberian kingdoms, dividing the New World among them giving each the responsibility and the authority to administer the mission work and the church in their new territories.

1492, October 12: Cristoforo Colombo reached Central America on behalf of Spain.

1494: Treaty of Tordesillas rearranged the boundaries between Portugal and Spain for the control of the New World.

1495-1425: King Manuel I ruled Portugal.

1497: Departure from Lisbon of Vasco de Gama for India, landing in Calicut in 1498. He started a Portuguese colony in Cochin in 1502.

1500-1502: Journey of Pedro Alvares Cabral to Brazil and India.

1502-1510: Travels of Ludovico da Barthema (who published a report in Rome, 1510).

1503: Pope Pius III (September 22 - October 18, 1503).

1503-1513: Pope Julius II (November 1, 1503 - February 21, 1513).

1503: The Chaldean Catholicos Simon sent three monks ordained bishops to 'the country of India, to the islands of the sea which are inside Java, and to China', according to a Syrian document, dated 1504.

1506-1521: Zhengde Emperor in China.

1510: Portuguese conquered and settled in Goa.

1511: After reaching Sumatra in 1508, the Portuguese Alfonso de Albuquerque conquered Malacca (present Melaka, on the western coast of Malaysia).

1512, December 27: Laws of Burgos, with Amendments on July 28, 1513.

1513-1521: Pope Leo X (March 11, 1513 - December 1, 1521).

1513 May: The Portuguese Jorge Alvares left Malacca and reached the coast of China, the island of Tamão, called "the island of the trade' = 'veniaga'; he was followed, in 1515, by Raphael Perestrello, "to discover China".

1514, January 12: Funchal, on Madeira Island and capital of Azores Islands, was created diocese with jurisdiction up to India and all areas discovered by Portuguese, under a bishop who resided in Lisbon.

1516: After the death of Ferdinand king of Spain, his daughter Joanna inherited the throne together with her son Charles I (the future Emperor of the Roman Empire Charles V), who ruled until his death (January 16, 1556).

1517, October 31: Martin Luther (1483-1546) wrote 'The 95 Theses', which gave origin to the 'Protestant Reformation'.

1519-1521: the Spaniards, led by Hernan Cortés (1485-1547), conquered the Aztec state in Mexico, which became the gateway of Spain to the Far East.

1519-1521: The first Spanish expedition to the Far East (reaching the Philippine Islands), led by Fernand Magellan.

1521: the Portuguese envoy, Tomé Pires, arrived in Peking.

1521-1566: Jiajing Emperor in China.

1522-1523: Pope Adrian VI (January 9, 1522 - September 14, 1523).

1523-1534: Pope Clement VII (November 18, 1523 - September 25, 1534): a member of the powerful Medici family, he possessed great political and diplomatic skills.

1525-1557: João III, king of Portugal.

1525: Second Spanish expedition to the Far East led by Juan Garcia Jofre de Loaysa, followed by a third by Alvaro Saavedra (1527).

1529, April 5: Treaty of Zaragoza between King John II of Portugal and the Emperor Charles V of Spain to define the areas of Spanish and Portuguese influence in the Far East.

1533, January 31: Goa was separated from Funchal diocese and established as diocese extending to Japan.

1534-1549: Pope Paul III (October 12, 1534 - November 10, 1549): he was the first pope of the Counter Reformation, inaugurating the Council of Trent on December 13, 1545 until September 17, 1547 (1st stage with 10 sessions).

1534, August 15: Ignace de Loyola with Francis Xavier and other companions joined together and founded the Society of Jesus, in Paris. It was approved by Pope Paul II on September 27, 1540, with the Bull *Regimini militantis Ecclesiae*.

1535: Portuguese seamen reached Lampacao, south of Macau, and later, Shangchuan Island.

1537: Paul III's Bull, *Sublimis Deus*, proclaimed the Indians rational beings.

1542, November 20: New Laws of the Indies, issued by Spain, with Amendments in 1543 and 1544,

1542-1543: Portuguese ships reached Japan.

1542-1544: A fourth Spanish expedition to the Far East led by Ruy Lopez de Villalobos, which failed by reaching the Moluccas.

1546: Francis Xavier, in a letter dated May 10, 1546 from Amboina (Ambon) one of the islands of the Moluccas, wrote about a possible presence of Christians in China.

1548: The Portuguese settlement near Ningbo, which had a good community of Catholics under the care of Fr. Estavão Nogueira, was destroyed by the Chinese fleet.

1550-1551: Junta of Valladolid, the public debate wanted by Charles V, between Bartolomé de Las Casas and Juan Ginès de Sepulveda, on the legitimacy of the Spanish conquest.

1550-1555: Pope Julius III (February 8, 1550 - March 23, 1555): he reopened the Council of Trent, from May 1, 1551 to April 23, 1552 (2nd stage with 6 sessions).

1552: Death of St Francis Xavier on the island of Shangchuan, just south of Macao.

1553: First settlement of Portuguese in Macao, among whom there were traders and a priest, Gregorio Gonzalez. It was settled in 1554 by a verbal compromise between Lionel de Souse and Wang Po.

1555: Pope Marcellus II (April 9, 1555 - May 1, 1555).

1555-1559: Pope Paul IV (May 23, 1555 - August 18, 1559).

1556 January 16 – 1598 September 13: Philip II ruled as king of Spain (from April 1581, also as Philip I king of Portugal).

1556, January 17-24: great earthquakes in various parts of China.

1556: Fr. Melchior Nunez Barreto, on his trip from India to Japan (started in 1554), via Malacca, in summer 1556, went to Canton and Macau.

1556 (end): A month stay in Canton (Guangzhou) of the Portuguese Dominican Gaspar da Cruz, who in 1569-70, published the *"Tractado das Cousas da China"* (Lisboa: Evora).

1556-1606: Reign of Mughal Emperor Akbar the Great in North India.

1557, February 4: Goa was raised to archdiocese with suffragan dioceses of Cochin and Malacca (which extended to China up to Japan)

1557-1578: Sebastião I, ruled as king of Portugal, followed by the rule of Cardinal Henrique. (1578-1580).

1560: The Jesuit Fr. Balthasar Gago, on his way from Japan to India, was thrown by a storm on the Island Hainan and remained there five months. He was sent to Macau, and then, via Malacca, reached India at Easter 1562.

1559-1565: Pope Pius IV (December 25, 1559 - December 9, 1565): he reconvened the Council of Trent on January 18, 1562 until December 4, 1563 (3rd stage with 9 sessions).

1563: Arrival at Macau of the Portuguese delegation to China, led by Diogo Pereira and Gil Gois. Diogo Pereira became *capitão mor*.

1564: The headquarters of the viceroy or governor of the Two Guangs (Guangdong and Guangxi moved from Wuzhou to Zhaoqing.

1564, 21 November: The Spanish expedition of Miguel Lopez de Legazpi left Mexico reaching Cebu on 26 April 1565, starting the Spanish conquest of the future Philippine islands (he occupied Manila in April 1571).

1565: Two Jesuit, Frs. Perez and Texeira opened the first Jesuit house in Macau.

1566-1572: Longqing Emperor in China.

1566-1572: Pope St. Pius V (January 1, 1566 - May 1, 1572).

1567: Bishop Melchior Carneiro, appointed second coadjutor of the Patriarch of Ethiopia, arrived in Macau, delegated by the Pope to exercise ministry in China and Japan.

1572-1585: Pope Gregory XIII (May 14, 1572 - April 10, 1585).

1572 August – 1580 August: Guido de Lavezares, Spanish Governor of the Philippines.

1573-1619: Wanli Emperor in China.

1575, 12 June - 28 October: Embassy of the Augustinian fathers Martin de Rada (1538-1578) and Jeronimo Marin to Fujian, due to the presence of the Chinese pirate, Limahon, who arrived in the Philippines on November 30, 1574.

1575, August 25 – 1580, April: Francisco de Sande, 3rd Governor of the Philippines.

1576: Second trip of Frs. Rada and Albuquerque to China, sent by Governor Francisco de Sande, but turned into failure.

1576, January 23: The Diocese of Macau was formally separated from that of Malacca and made autonomous, covering the whole of the Far East (China, Mongolia, Korea and Japan), with Bishop Diego Nunez de Figuerosa, who however was substituted by Bishop Fernandes de Sa (on October 27, 1579, arriving in Macau in 1581).

1577: Arrival in the Philippines of the first 15 Franciscans led by Fr. Pedro de Alfaro.

1579, June 15: First journey to China of the Franciscan friars, led by Pedro de Alfaro (until September).

1580 April – 1583 March 10: Gonzalo Ronquillo de Penalosa, Spanish Governor of the Philippines.

1580-1581: Embassy sent by king Philip II from Spain of Augustinian Fathers Jeronimo Marin, Francisco Ortega and Juan Gonzales de Mendoza, but soon dissolved in Mexico.

1581, April 15: Philip II is accepted as king of Portugal (union of the crowns of Spain and Portugal).

1581, 17 September: Arrival at Manila of its first bishop, the Dominican Bishop Domingo de Salazar, appointed by Gregory XIII on 6 February 1578, together with his confrere Fr Christoval de Salvatierra, and the first Jesuits Frs. Pedro Sedeno and Alonso Sanchez.

1582, 14 March: The Jesuit Fr. Alonso Sanchez was sent to Macao as ambassador from the Philippines governor Gonzalo Ronquillo to solicit the acceptance of Philip II as king of both Spain and Portugal, from the local Portuguese community and to obtain a trading port from China.

1582, June 21: From Manila, the second journey to China of seven Franciscans led by the Visitor Commissar, Fray Jeronimo de Burgos.

1583, February 13: Fr. Sanchez and some Franciscans left Macau.

1583 March 10 – 1584 May 16: Diego Ronquillo, acting Governor of the Philippines.

1583: An expedition of eight Franciscans to Indochina (Vietnam), which however ended up, due to contrary winds, in Hainan Island, led by Fr. Didace de Oropesa.

1583, September 10: Frs. Michel Ruggieri e Matteo Ricci arrived in Zhaoqing and started a lasting Catholic presence in China.

1584 April: The *Factor Real* (Royal Factor) Juan Batista Roman and Fr. Sanchez returned to Macao in search of the galleon San Juan (arriving on May 1 to October 1, 1584) and to arrange an eventual Spanish embassy to China.

1584 May 16 – 1590 May: Dr. Santiago de Vera, Spanish Governor of the Philippines.

1585, 28 January: The Jesuits obtained from Gregory XIII with the Brief *Ex Pastorali Officio* (28 January 1585) the exclusive right for the evangelization of Eastern Asia.

1585: Publication of the book *"Historia del gran Reyno de China"* by the Augustinian Juan Gonzalez de Mendoza (Madrid, Pedro Madrigal Printer, 1586) in I Part (3 books) and II Part (2 books + Itinerary of Franciscan Priests).

1585-1590: Pope Sixtus V (April 24, 1585 - August 27, 1590).

1586, April 20: The *Audencia,* o general assembly of Manila was held in Manila, whose members signed the Memorial to the Council of the Indies (with various proposals, among which that of *La Empresa de China*).

1586, 15 November: Pope Sixtus V, in the brief *"Dum ad uberes fructus"* raised the Custodia into the Franciscan Province of Saint Gregory in the Philippines, and granted permission to found convents in the West Indies and in the Kingdom of China).

1586: The Augustinians Frs. Juan B. de Montoya and Francisco Manrique from Manila reached Macau and founded a convent. In the following year, they were joined by Frs. Diego de Espinar, Nicolas de Tolentino and Luis Arias, from the Philippines. However, they had to cede it to the Portuguese missionaries in 1596.

1587, September 17: Arrival in the Philippines of the first official group of other 14 Dominicans led by the vicar general, Fr. Juan Castro.

1588: Diocese of Funay (Japan) was separated from the diocese of Macau.

1588, November 25: Fr. Valignano sent Fr. Ruggieri back to Europe to arrange an embassy of the Holy See to China.

1589, August 9: King Philip forbade religious clergy from the Philippines to go to China and establish convents in Macau.

1590 June – 1593 October 25: Gomez Pereira Dasmariñas, Governor of the Philippines (until his murder by Chinese seamen).

1590: Pope Urban VII (September 15-27, 1590).

1590-1591: Pope Gregory XIV (December 5, 1590 - October 16, 1591).

1590: Expedition to China of the Dominican Fathers, Juan de Castro and Miguel de Benavides from Manila, but with failure.

1591: Pope Innocent IX (October 29 - December 30, 1591).

1592-1605: Pope Clement VIII (January 30, 1592 – March 5, 1605).

1592: The Dominican province of the Holy Rosary was established.

1593: Another embassy left Manila, composed of Don Francisco de Castro and the Dominican Fathers Luis Gandullo and Juan de Castro, they headed for Fujian, in search of the murderers of governor Dom Gomez Perez Dasmariñas.

1593 December 3 – 1595 June 11: Luiz Perez Dasmariñas, acting governor of Manila.

1595, February 18: King Philip II allowed only Jesuits and Franciscans to work in Macau.

1596-1602: Francisco de Tello de Guzman, Spanish governor of the Philippines.

1597, August 4: Fr. Matteo Ricci was appointed Superior of the Jesuit Mission in China.

1597, December 20: The Jesuit Superior General, Fr. Claudio Acquaviva, opposed a Pontifical Embassy to China, although Jesuit missionaries insisted on the plan (in 1599 and 1600) until Fr. Alessandro Valignano also agreed to give it up on October 21, 1600.

1598-1599: The Spaniards obtained from the Chinese authorities a trading port, between Canton and Macao, called 'El Pinal' (Pine Grove).

1598-1621: Philip III (Philip II) ruled as king of Spain and Portugal.

1600: Pope Clement VIII issued the Constitution *Onerosa pastoralis*, which allowed missionaries of all congregation and countries to go to Japan and China.

1606, January 20: Death of Fr. Valignano in Macao.

1610, May 11: Death of Fr. Matteo Ricci in Beijing,

1614: Publication of *Peregrinacão,* by Fernand Mendez Pinto (translated by H. Cogan in 1663, The Voyages and Adventures of Ferdinand Mendez Pinto).

1621-1627: Tianqi Emperor in China.

1622, January 6: Pope Gregory XV established the Sacred Congregation for the Evangelization of Peoples (or Propaganda Fide).

1632, 22 February: Urban VIII's Bull concerning Missions (issued by the Pontifical Legate to Spain, on 28 June 1633).

1
THE SOCIAL AND POLITICAL CONTEXT IN THE XVI CENTURY

The 'Impact' of the Geographical Discoveries

Francisco López de Gómara, a mid-sixteenth century Spanish historian, stated that: *The greatest event since the creation of the world (excluding the incarnation and death of Him who created it) is the discovery of the Indies.* [1] 'Indies', at that time, were identified with all the mysterious New World, that is, lands both in the West and in the East, that travelers, among whom Marco Polo, have spoken of. Consequently, their populations were called "Indians". Later on, when geographical knowledge improved, people differentiated between Eastern and Western Indies.

The 'discovery' of the New World was indeed an eye-opener for the outlook of Europe and constituted a strong push toward new horizons, especially by Portuguese and Spanish explorers: it opened new avenues and opportunities for trade and exchanges with foreign lands, putting Europe really in the 'global' context.

However, it was indeed a rather inexplicable and strange fact! Europe already possessed a great quantity of knowledge about Asia, but it seemed it has forgotten it.

"Since 1310 and perhaps even before", - notes A. T'Serstevens — "thousands of people in Europe were acquainted with the 'things of China'. Only to mention the Popes and their entourage, several kings of the West and their courts, the superiors of the religious orders, monks and friars who had returned from there, the merchants from Italy and other countries, who in their trading contacts had financed the building of churches…, we already gather a group of persons of a certain importance, both for their quality and for their number. No one of these people, probably only except the merchants, had any motivation to hide their knowledge about that distant country. Everybody, on the contrary, should have rejoiced to know that the

---

[1] Quoted in J.H. Elliot, *The Old World and the New, 1492-1650* (Cambridge: At the University Press, 1969), p. 10.

Catholic faith was spreading there. And yet, the geographers continued to ignore it. The Central and Oriental Asia, known by many people, remained a mystery only for the learned people!" [2]

The beginning of the 'discoveries' dates earlier in the fifteenth century when the Portuguese had started to conduct exploratory voyages down along the coast of Africa. Such an enterprise finds its roots, when the Portuguese Order of the Knights of Christ (*Ordo Militiae Christi*, a religious order of soldiers-monks [3]) had accepted the ideological inheritance and the properties of the suppressed Order of the Temple of Jerusalem (or Templars) and had been approved by Pope John XXII with his Bull *Ad ea ex quibus* (14-15 March, 1319). The Bull is not only the Magna Charta of the Order of the Knights of Christ, but also the basis of Portugal's future colonial expansion and its ecclesiastical jurisdiction in the conquered territories, the *real padroado,* as we later will see in details.

The motivations that pushed the Portugal to extend its empire are well summarized by the Encyclopedia Britannica in these terms:

"The idea of expansion into Africa was a logical result of the completion of the reconquest in the peninsula, and the conquest of Ceuta in North Africa (1415) probably provided the impulse toward further expansion, The simple idea of fighting the Muslims on their own soil was linked with more complicated motives: the desire to explore in a scientific sense, the hope of finding a way to the rich spice trade of the Indies, and the impulse to spread the Christian faith. These purposes were gradually molded together into a national enterprise, though at first, they represented the hopes and aspirations of one man, Prince Henry..." [4]

---

[2] A. T'Serstevens, *I Precursori di Marco Polo* (Milano: Garzanti 1982), pp. 52-53.

[3] After the Order of the Temple (Templars)'s suppression by Pope Clement in 1312 (it was founded around 1118), King Denis of Portugal set about creating a new order for the displaced knights in his realm. He instituted the "*Christi Militia*" in 1317 (some sources say August 14, 1318), and Pope John XXII approved this order by the Bull on March 14, 1319 *Ad ea ex quibus*. After four years of negotiations, the same Pope passed another bull authorizing Denis to grant the Templar's property to the Order of the Knights of Christ in 1323. In 1357, the Order was moved from Castro Marim, in the Algarve, to the town of Tomar, near Santarém, former seat of the Order of the Knights of the Temple in Portugal.

[4] Encyclopedia Britannica (Macropedia), *Portugal, History of,* (William Benton Publisher 1943-1973), vol. 14, p. 868.

A world-wide perspective will provide a more pluralistic and complex picture of human life and society in the XVI century.

While Spain and Portugal explored and conquered the world seas, with Latin America becoming a Spanish colony, and Portugal the master of the Indian Ocean, snatching the control from the Arab hands, as we will see in details, China, during and after the 1405-1433 seven sea expeditions of Zheng He (Ma He1371-1433), decided for an isolation policy officially forbidding its subjects from emigrating or trading overseas, on pain of death. The ban however was not strictly kept, and junks from Fujian and Guangdong continued to sail to Malayan, Indochinese and Indonesian ports for trading purposes. Due to the prohibition, they frequently were considered and often were acting as pirates, conniving with the Japanese pirates (*wako*), first and later, with Portuguese merchant-adventurers. So, the Chinese authorities became very concerned with protecting the coastal areas from the local and Japanese piracy. Japan, in that period, was suffering under a severe civil war.

"Official relations with Japan could only be conducted through the port of Ningbo, at the north-eastern tip of Chekiang; Fuzhou was reserved for trade with the Philippines and a similar role had been assumed later by Quanzhou. In 1530 permission for the Japanese to send missions to Ningbo was withdrawn. From that moment onwards piracy made rapid progress, and more and more recruits began to come from China itself. The pirates' principal bases were in the Chusan Islands off the north-east coast of Chekiang, and in Xiamen (Amoy) and Quanzhou area, in Chaozhou area (north-east of Kwangtung)." [5]

In the Middle East, the Ottoman Empire was quite dynamic, with the Arabs in control of the trade in the Pacific Ocean, while in the Indian region, Mughal Emperor Akbar the Great (1542-1605), was ruling rather opulently and trying to achieve good harmony in the country by reconciling the major religions in a syncretistic way.

---

[5] For more details, see Jacques Granet, *A History of Chinese Civilization* (Cambridge: Cambridge University Press 1989), pp. 420-422.

The Portuguese Empire

Portugal, as a nation, dates its origin on 24 June 1128. Alfonso proclaimed himself the first *King of Portugal* in 1139. By 1143, Portugal was formally recognized as independent. From 1249 to 1250, Algarve, the southernmost region, was finally re-conquered from the Moors (as Muslims were then called), who had invaded the Iberic peninsula since the beginning of the 8th century.

The success of the liberation of the Iberic peninsula from the Muslim and the lingering feeling of hostility towards them due to their piratical raids on the Mediterranean coasts, combined with the spirit of adventure, were quite lively in the family of King John I of Portugal (1357-1433, r. from 1385), especially in one of his sons, Prince Henry (1394-1460, later called 'the Navigator'). Both men decided to build up a fleet and depart for the rich Muslim city of Ceuta, in North Africa, conquering it on August 21, 1415. Thus, the Portuguese Empire was started. Prince Henry's interest in exploration with some technological developments in navigation improved Portugal's fleet and led to the expansion of its empire, together with great advances in geographic and scientific knowledge.

John I, not satisfied with having taken the town of Ceuta, resolved to continue the fight against the Muslims, in order to propagate both the Portuguese empire and the Christian faith. Pope Martin V (r. 1417-1431), desirous of aiding him in this enterprise, urged all the Christian princes to share the dangers that John was about to run.

On May 25, 1420, Prince Henry was appointed as the great Prior or Master of the Order of the Knights of Christ, holding this position until his death. The Order was an important source of funds for Henry's enterprises. In 1419, his Portuguese sailors discovered Madeira Islands, followed by the Azores in 1427.

In 1433, Pope Eugene IV awarded "all the islands, conquered and to be conquered" to the Portuguese Order of the Knights of Christ. On June 18, 1452, Pope Nicholas V allowed the king Alphonse V of Portugal ('the African', 1432-1481, r. from 1438), with the Bull *Dum Diversas*, to make war to the infidels, in view of their conversion and, if not, reducing "Saracens and pagans" into slavery. On January 8, 1454, with the Bull *Romanus Pontifex*, the same Pope affirmed to the King Alfonse and Prince Henry the right of the Portuguese to the conquest and occupation as 'perpetual possession' of all lands of the unbelievers, that might be discovered along the West coast of Africa.

In 1456 Pope Callixtus III entrusted to Prince Henry and to the Order of the Knights of Christ, the spiritual care over all the existing dominions of the Crown of Portugal, and over any that might in the future be added to them. By 1462, the Portuguese had explored the coast of Africa as far as the present Sierra Leone.

On October 10, 1486 King John II (1455-1495, r. from 1481) of Portugal appointed Bartolomeu Dias (1450-1500) to lead an expedition to sail to the southern tip of Africa and try to contact the supposedly Christian ruler, known as 'Prester John'[6], king of Ethiopia, about whom so many rumors have been circulated for so long that he has become a 'legend'. In August 1587, Dias departed from Lisboa. The travel lasted sixteen months, passing Angola and in January 1588 reaching the '*Cabo tormentoso*' (Cape of storms, later called 'Cape of Good Hope'). He sailed up along the coast until the Fish River, to the present Kwaaihoek (in present South Africa), from where he started the journey back home (March 12, 1588) reaching Lisboa in December.

Portugal's further discoveries in Asia

In July 1497, from Lisbon, Vasco de Gama (ca.1460s - 1524), accompanied by 170 men among whom Bartolomeu Dias, departed for India, landing in Calicut (modern Kozhikode) on May 20, 1498. Negotiations with the ruler of Calicut, took on a violent nature. Efforts by Gama to obtain favorable trade terms were complicated by resistance from Arab merchants. Eventually Gama was able to gain a concession for trading rights. He left a few Portuguese with orders to start a trading post, and sailed to Lisboa in August 1498.

---

[6] The legend of the 'Prester John (Presbyter Johannes), a Christian Priest-King, who was said to rule a Christian kingdom amidst the pagan world, was quite popular from the XII to the XVII century in Europe. His kingdom was located in different places, from India, to Central Asia, North China, East Africa, etc. The Portuguese explorers were rightly convinced about its location in Ethiopia.

The year 1500 registered the voyage to Brazil and to India of Pedro Alvares Cabral (1467-1520) with Bartolomeu Dias. When Cabral finally reached India, he learned that the Portuguese citizens who had been left by Gama had been murdered. After encountering further resistance from the locals, he attacked Calicut; then, he sailed south reaching Cochin, a small kingdom where he was given a warm welcome. Cabral returned to Portugal on June 23, 1501, with only four of the original 13 ships, lost in a storm around the Cape of Good Hope (Bartolomeu Dias lost his life), but with silk and gold.

On February 12, 1502, Vasco da Gama again sailed with the purpose of enforcing Portuguese interests in the East. He first engaged some fights on the East African coasts, then under Arab control. He reached Calicut on October 30, 1502. His ships engaged first against Arab ships, and then attacked a Calicut fleet. Following the victory, he extracted favorable trading concessions from the local ruler. He returned to Portugal, in September 1503.

In 1503, Afonso de Albuquerque (1453-1515) set out on his first expedition to India. He succeeded in establishing the king of Cochin securely on his throne, obtaining in return for this service permission to build a Portuguese fort at Cochin, and thus laying the foundation of his country's empire in the East. Albuquerque returned home in July 1504.

Meanwhile, in 1503 King Manuel I of Portugal (1469-1521, r. from 1495) appointed Francisco de Almeida (1450-1510) as viceroy of *Estado da Índia*. With an armada of 22 ships, Almeida departed from Lisbon in March 1505. The mission's primary aims were to bring the spice trade under Portuguese control, to construct forts along the east African and Indian coasts, to foster alliances with local rulers, and open trading ports. Almeida rounded the Cape of Good Hope and proceeded northwards to the coastal settlement of Kilwa. In July 1505 he conquered this town. Due to the good conditions of its harbor, the Portuguese built a fort, and left there a crew of 80 soldiers. In August 1505 Almedia arrived at Mombasa, a coastal port further north, which was conquered in a heavy combat against the troops of the local Arab sheiks. The same month a caravel of Almeida's fleet captured Zanzibar Island. After reaching India, Almeida took up residence in Cochin. He strengthened the Portuguese fortifications in the area. In March 1506 his son Lourenço de Almeida won a sea battle at the entrance to the harbor of Cannamore, and then he explored the southern coasts of Sri Lanka.

In 1506, Tristão da Cunha (ca. 1460-1540) was entrusted by the Portuguese king with a fleet of 15 ships in order to operate on the eastern coasts of Africa and of India. Afonso de Albuquerque was in charge of a squadron in this fleet and subsequently detached his ships under royal orders to attack the island of Hormuz, in the Persian Gulf, which was then one of the chief centers of commerce in the East. He reached the place in September 1507, and soon took possession of the island; though he was unable to maintain his position for long, he could build a fort on the island. Then he reached Cochin at the close of 1508 and immediately made known the secret commission he had received from the King empowering him to supersede Governor Almeida. Almeida refused to recognize Albuquerque's credentials and arrested him. Albuquerque was released after three-month confinement.

Meanwhile, earlier in 1509, Almeida became the first Portuguese to set sail in Bombay. His fleet inflicted a decisive defeat on the joint fleet of Arabs, Egyptians and Indians in the naval Battle of Diu in February 1509. The victory marked the beginning of Portuguese hegemony in the Indian Ocean, which was to last into the 17th century.

Almeida having returned home, Albuquerque speedily showed the energy and determination of his character, as the second viceroy of the *Estado da India*, a position he would hold until his death. Albuquerque intended to dominate the Muslim world and control the spices trading network. In 1510, he attacked Goa, and conquered it. But unable to hold the town, abandoned it in August to return with the reinforcements in November, when he obtained undisputed possession. In April 1511, he set sail from Goa to Malacca with a force of some 1200 men and 17 ships. He conquered Malacca on August 24, 1511, after a severe struggle throughout July. Albuquerque remained in Malacca until December 1511 preparing its defense against any Malay counterattack. Knowing of the ambitions of the king of Siam (Thailand) over Malay, Albuquerque immediately sent a diplomatic mission to establish friendly relations between Portugal and Siam. In November 1511, he ordered the first Portuguese ships to sail eastward in search of the Spice Islands of Moluccas (Maluku): the expedition reached Banda Islands and Moluccas, and established Ternate as the center of their further contacts in the area (1513). In September 1512, Albuquerque could reach Goa, after meeting a violent storm at the coast of Malabar. There he took such measures for the security and peace of the town that it became the most flourishing of the Portuguese settlements in India.

Portuguese Contacts with China

In May 1513, Jorge Alvares (+ 1521), under the order of the first captain of Malacca, Rui de Brito Patalim, left for the coasts of China and reached them in June 1513, starting a settlement on Tamão island, "the island of trade" (*'veniaga'*), in the estuary area of the Xijiang and Zhujiang (West and Pearl Rivers), where he raised a *padrão* pillar as a sign of possession.[7] One year and a half later, in 1515, the same island was reached by the Italian Raphael Perestrello, from Malacca with about a dozen of Portuguese sailors. They went on to Canton (Guangzhou), and returned to Malacca in autumn 1516, with the good information about the friendliness of the Chinese. This news convinced the Viceroy of India, Albuquerque, to send Tomé Pires[8] as ambassador to China with Fernão Peres de Andrade as chief of the expedition of several ships (June 1517). From Tamão they reached Canton in September 1517, kindly welcomed by the Chinese officials. From there, Fernão Peres sent Jorge Mascareñhas to explore the Ryu Kyu (Liu Qiu) Islands but he could reach only Fujian, stopping at *Chincheu* (present Bay of Xiamen, with the two cities of Zhangzhou and Quanzhou). Then, he was recalled back by Fernão Peres, who remained in Canton until September 1518 and returned to Malacca. So, Tomé Pires could leave Canton for Nanjing on January 23, 1520, and reached Beijing in 1521.

However, in the meantime, the good efforts of Fernão Peres de Andrade to establish a solid relationship between China and Portugal were destroyed by his brother Simão de Andrade. The latter, with a fleet had reached Tamão in August 1519, where he built a fort under the pretext of defense against pirates, and started to launch attacks against Chinese junks. The local offi-

---

[7] Some scholars set the journey of Jorge Alvares in 1514. The location of the "Tamão island" is disputed: some scholars identify it with Hachuan (Montaldo de Jesus, in Historic Macao, p. 3-11), others with Shangchuan island nearby, where St. Francis Xavier died in 1552 (The Chinese Repository, Dec. 1856, p. 346; Carlos J. Caldeira), others locate it in the area of Namtau and the harbor of Tun Mun (the Dongguan Gazetteer), identifying it with Lingding island (José M. Braga and Manuel Texeira).

[8] Tomé Pires (1465? – 1524 or 1540): he went to India in 1511 and in 1515 he published the *Suma Oriental,* a well- documented geography treatise of countries along the coasts of Asia.

cials sent complaints to Beijing. Moreover, there the ambassador of Bintan,[9] son of the king of Malacca, deposed by the Portuguese, also complained against them. The death of Zhengde Emperor on April 19, 1521, and accusations against the Portuguese convinced the Ming court to send Tomé Pires and his followers back to Canton, where they were put into prison,[10] and ordered to eliminate all the *Ferangi*,[11] the foreigners, in Guangdong. This led to the first conflict between China and Portugal, the battle of Tunmen in 1521. The new envoy Martin Alfonso de Mello Coutinho, who arrived in 1522, lost great party of his escort in the second conflict with the Chinese fleet at Xicaowan in 1522.[12]

After these defeats, the Portuguese looked for other places. In the South they started to stop at Shangchuan and northwards, besides Wuyu island, in the Xiamen Bay already in contact, they reached the Zhushan archipelago, in Ningbo area,[13] where they set a smuggling center at Double-Island anchorage (Shuangyugang), very prosperous during the decades 1526-1548, due to a good connivance with Chinese and Japanese smugglers or pirates.

According to Mendez Pinto, in 1542, in Ningbo area there was a Portuguese community of 1,200 members, but the settlement seems to have

---

[9] Bintan is the largest of 3,200 islands in the Riau Archipelago, and is located at about 40 kilometers from Singapore. Bintan first became politically important when Sultan of Malacca fled there and built up a resistance base after Malacca was taken by the Portuguese forces in 1511.

[10] Tomé was forced to write letters to Malacca stating that he and other ambassadors would not be released from prison in China until the Portuguese relinquished their control of Malacca and returned it to its deposed Sultan, who was a Ming tributary vassal. Some of his followers were executed, others died of hardship, while two of them, Christovao Vieria and Vasco Calvo, succeeded in smuggling out letters which recorded their plight.

[11] Feranji (or Ferenji in Arabic, firang in Persian with similar words appearing in Hindi, Urdu, Chinese 佛郎機 Folangji…) refers to foreigners, from 'Franks', the name with which all foreigners were called since the Crusades, by the Arabs and Persians: it spread in all languages of South East Asia and Far East countries.

[12] About details on the date and location of the battle of Xicaowan, see Lin Tien-wei, An Enquiry into the Portuguese Stay in Hong Kong during the Sixteenth Century, in *Chinese Culture*, vol. XXV, No. 4, December 1984, pp. 65-101.

[13] For further details on the Portuguese presence in Ningbo, see "Wang Mumin Shiliu, shiqishiji Putoaya yu Ningbo zhiguanxi (Relationship between Portugal and Ningbo in the 16th and 17th centuries)" in *Journal of Macao Studies*, No. 10, 1999, 3, pp. 1-31.

been smaller, with at most few hundreds of people among Portuguese, African and local servants. Due to the Chinese decision of getting rid of all smugglers, in June 1548, according to the Chinese records, all the establishments were tragically destroyed: all people were dispersed or lost their life, the buildings burnt down.[14] The Portuguese merchants continued to make use of the bay of Xiamen, where their establishment suffered the same sort of those in Ningbo in 1549).[15] Prisoners were taken by the Chinese, some of whom were executed some others put into prison (among then Galeote Pereira, who, in the meantime had reached Zoumaxi, half way between Shantou and Xiamen, and was captured in March 1549, but he could escaped in 1553 to Shangchuan and wrote about his experience). This however did not prevent further contacts, both as traders and smugglers, often in cooperation with Japanese pirates.

---

[14] "No proof has yet emerged of Pinto's story of this settlement's sudden destruction in 1542, and it appears to have died slowly" (John King Fairbank, *Trade and Diplomacy on the China Coast*, Stanford University Press, 1969, p. 328). However, Chinese records and recent studies by Chinese scholars prove the event (see Wang Mumin, a.c., in *Journal of Macao Studies*, 10, 1999, 3, pp. 1-31).

[15] José S. Arcilla, "Alonso Sanchez: Jesuit Diplomat to the Portuguese in Macao" (in A.N. Baxter at alii, eds., *Conference Proceedings of Macao-Philippines Historical Relations*, Macao: Universidade de Macao & CEPESA, 2005, p. 159) provides the occasions of the Chinese action in both places, but without quoting the source: *"In 1542, Lanzarote Pereira arrived in Liampo [Ningbo] and entered into a business arrangement worth 1,000 gold pieces with the Chinese. When the latter failed to reappear and pay the loan, Pereira in his anger attacked even innocent Chinese of the village of Lipton about 10 kilometers away. In retaliation, the Imperial Prefect and Viceroy ordered the destruction of Liampo, killing 12 Christian soldiers and burning 800 Portuguese. Seventy-seven boats with their merchandise (gold, silver, spices, sandalwood) were captured, and the Portuguese expelled. With handsome gifts and bribes, the Portuguese were able to secure another foothold in Chincheo. One of them, Aria Botello, who had brought back Lanzarote, became magistrate in charge of the estates of the deceased. An Armenian trader, Luis Montergogo, died leaving an estate worth 12,000 ducats. Chinese merchants, meantime, arrived to pay the dead man 2,000 ducats, the profit from their trade. Botello took charge, promising to send money to the dead man's heirs in Armenia. Botello should have stopped there, but he accused the Chinese of dishonesty for refusing to pay a much bigger debt to their Armenian partner. The Chinese appealed to their Viceroy, who banned his subjects from further dealings with the Portuguese, took over 12 Portuguese ships and only 30 were saved from the vengeance exacted on Botello's criminal plans."*

22

In the meantime, in the South, the Portuguese not only continued to stop in Shangchuan island, but from 1535, reached also Lampacao,[16] few miles northward. They merely built mat-sheds ashore for the duration of the trading season. At Shangchuan, since 1550 they could hold a yearly commercial fair, transferred to Lampacao by the captain-major Leonnel de Sousa in 1554. Here in 1555 a colony of 5-600 Portuguese lived around a chapel.

In 1542-43 Portuguese ships started to reach Japan.

The Portuguese landed in Macao probably in 1553, where Leonel de Sousa reached a verbal compromise with Wang Po, the acting commander of the coastguard fleet at the end of 1554, allowing to trade in Guangdong on the same terms as the Siamese.[17]

"As the news of the peace – wrote the secular priest Gregorio Gonzales few years later, [18] - *I was sent* [as delegate of the vicar general of Malacca], *and for the first year I resided on the continent with seven Christians; the following year the Lord has opened my mind and so I converted some Chinese to the faith of Jesus Christ, still residing on shore in a chapel thatched with straw…"*

However, after the departure of the Portuguese ships, the priest and his Christians were caught by the Chinese officials, imprisoned and sent to different places, without knowing the destination of one another, accused of residing on land in order to hatch some treason.

"They detained us until next year. Then, we came together again [in Macau] *and I built another church and the Portuguese some houses. Since then, I resided there,*

---

[16] Lampacao (Longbakou), in Nanshui, former island, is in Chik-kai district, 18 miles south-west of Macao (Manuel Texeira), 'near the modern Bullock Horn Island, at six leagues from Macao' (C.R. Boxer); Lin Tien-wei, in the article quoted above, locates it on Taiyushan or Lantao Island, in the present Hong Kong Special Administrative Region. The first location is the right one, although traces of a Portuguese presence remain also on Lantau Island.

[17] See his letter dated January 15, 1555, published by J.M. Braga, *Western Pioneers*, pp. 84-86, 202-208, and quoted by C. Boxer, *South China in the XVI century* (Hakluyt Society 1953, Kraus Reprint Limited 1967), p. xxxv.

[18] Quoted in C.R. Boxer, *South China…*, o.c, pp. xxxv-xxxvi, and in H. Bernard, *Aux Portes de la Chine, Les Missionaires du 16th siécle* (Tientsin, Haute Eudes, 1933), p. 9.

in contacts with the Chinese ever more pacific. I started to better understand the country and to baptize some Christians. I always took care that the people of the country should be helped and supported in their needs. I treated them myself, trying my best to treat them with equality."

The Chinese having thus known him, let him alone to continue quietly his missionary work for 12 years.[19]

Within these years the Portuguese built "a very large settlement on a point of the mainland, which is called Macao, with three churches and a hospital for the poor, and a House of the Santa Misericordia, which nowadays forms a settlement of over five thousand Christian souls." [20] Meanwhile, in 1556, Luis Vaz de Camoes (c. 1524-1580), one of Portugal's greatest poets, worked there as *provedor mor* (senior executor), responsible for administering the property of people who died or were missing. In 1557, the Portuguese started to build walled houses and to fortify the town. Thus, Macau became the main basis of their trading activities and further expansion, a meeting point for the Portuguese on their way to and from Canton.

But it took some years to consolidate its status. On 29 July 1563, the Portuguese diplomatic mission from India reached Macau, head by Diogo Pereira and Gil Goys, the former as ambassador of the king of Portugal to the emperor of China. Its purpose was to improve the relationship with the Chinese authorities and insure the future of Macau. However, in Macau Diogo was elected *capitão de terra* by the local citizens and preferred to keep this post and sent Gil Goys as ambassador with two Jesuits. In Canton, the Chinese authorities did not recognize the embassy and stopped it, limiting the negotiations to dealing with goods aimed at the Japanese market: they despised and opposed the diplomatic strategy adopted by Macanese traders.

When in 1581, the union of the crowns of Portugal and Spain under Philip II was established, the Governor of Manila, Don Gonzalo Ronquillo, as we will see, sent the Jesuit Fr. Alonso Sanchez, to promote the recognition of the new monarch in Macau: the Portuguese there remained suspicious of the Spanish motives in trade, politics and religion towards China, and, only with the agreement from Goa, they formally accepted the fact and

---

[19] M. Texeira, *The Fourth Centenary of the Jesuits at Macao* (Macao, 1964), p. 7.
[20] Ibid.

24

made the oath of alliance (on December 18, 1582). Soon after, in 1583, through the initiative of Bishop Melchior Carneiro, they established a local legislature, the *Senado da Camara*, to maintain the city's autonomy.

However, the existence of Macau depended upon Chinese consent. In 1583, the local Portuguese community complained about mandarins' harassing the merchants who traded with them, by means of extorting excessive taxation, restricting food supply and overcharging daily necessities. In fact, rather frequently mandarins sent vicious agents to Macau for the purpose of picking quarrels, so to justify their restrictions. Persistent popular opinion in Macau was that the Chinese wanted to chase away the Portuguese, but retaining control of the enclave was seen as vital to the Portuguese interests, since it was already becoming a major player in the commercial and religious activity of the region.

Spain and the Division of the world with Portugal

Early in XV century, Spain was divided in few reigns, of which the most powerful was Castille. Its army intervened in Northern Africa, competing with the Portuguese Empire, when Henry III of Castille began the colonization of the Canary Islands in 1402. The conquest of these Islands required from the armies of the Crown of Castille long and bloody wars. They were the islands of Gran Canaria (1478-1483), La Palma (1492-1493) and Tenerife (1494-1496). The marriage of the *Reyes Católicos* (Ferdinand II of Aragon and Isabella I of Castille) in 1469 created a confederation of reigns, each with their own administrations, but ruled by a common monarchy. A civil war begun in 1474 over the succession of the kingdom of Castille. The Treaty of Alcáçovas (4 September 1474) settled the question in favor of Isabella, as well as the disputes between Castille and Portugal over the control of the Atlantic. The treaty, ratified later by the Papal Bull *Aeterni Regis* in 1481, essentially gave the Portuguese free rein to continue their exploration along the African coasts, while guaranteeing Castillian sovereignty on the Canaries.

In 1479, with the effective rule of Ferdinand and Isabel the unity was achieved and 'España', with its empire was born. The first decade of their joint rule registered the conquest of the Kingdom of Granada, the last Arab-Muslim state in the Iberian Peninsula, which was completed by1492. In that same year, Christopher Columbus was sent by the royal couple on his expedition bound for East Asia, which resulted in the Spanish arrival in America.

King John II of Portugal obstinately maintained that all the New World, without any exception, belonged to him, in consequence of grants by previous Roman Pontiffs. But, the voyages of Columbus had been undertaken under the patronage of the Crown of Spain. Ferdinand, the king of Spain, therefore, supported his claim by a concession made to him by Pope Alexander VI (r. 1492-1503). In fact, the Pope, with the Bull *Inter Coetera* in 1493 had recognized

> *"the exclusive right of the Spanish crown to trade with land that had been or might be discovered to the west of the Atlantic, and at the same time laid on the king the injunction to bring to Christian faith the peoples who inhabit these islands and the mainland, and to send to the said islands and of the mainland wise, upright, God-fearing, and virtuous men who will be capable of instructing the indigenous peoples in good morals and in the Catholic faith."*

To avoid rivalry between the two powers, the Pope drew a line on the map from the North Pole to the South, and established that all the lands east of the imaginary pole-to-pole line passing 100 leagues (480 km) west of Cape Verde Islands, belonged to Portugal, and lands west of the line belonged to Spain. So, the New World was divided between the two Iberian sovereigns who were entrusted also with the responsibility and the authority to administer the mission work and establish the Church in the territories. With the Treaty of Tordesillas (1494), the two kings rearranged the boundaries of their control: the line was moved for 370 leagues (1,770 km) west of Cape Verde.

Vasco's discovery of a route to India and the Far East, independent of the Mediterranean Sea, opened a new era for trade to the East Indies, whose importance rivaled that of the West Indies. The European market was dramatically increased within the span of a few years. The new trade routes and the abundance of resources made available through these discoveries put Portugal and Spain at the center of an Atlantic-oriented trade network. It began to supplant the up to then dominant Mediterranean-based trade system, centered upon the predominance of Genoa and Venice together with the Turks in the trade between Europe and Asia. With the new route to the East around Africa, their monopoly was undercut. A lot of European trade was then channeled through Portugal and Spain along these new routes.[21]

The Empire of Spain

Spanish further colonial expansion developed from 1519, and within two years Hernan Cortez (1485-1547) conquered the Aztec state in Mexico, calling it Nueva España, the New Spain, which became the gateway to both South America and to the Far East.

The driving motivation was, indeed, the material benefits. However, the imperial conquest by Spain of Mexico and Peru was not simply the result of military pride, spirit of adventure and military force of the Spanish soldiers. As the prospects for gain became evident, the new monarchies and the financial establishments of Europe were quick to join in, outfitting exploratory voyages as well as providing the capital for the colonization. So, the way in which the conquests were carried out reflected new realities on the European scene.

Moreover, the Spaniards did not arrive in the New World simply to plunder and to get hold of its riches; they brought wives, they built cities, they settled permanently as residents of these lands, and carried much of "home" with them. Still the lust for gold was paramount, and they made use of the military force to subjugate lands and peoples. The spread of the Gospel was the formal legitimization of the conquest; but actually, the Church was subordinated to the civil government, a tool for its economic and political purposes.

"Queen Isabella had declared at the very beginning of the conquest that 'Castile possessed a just title to the Indies because of its obligation to evangelize the Indians, and, indeed, this was the sole justification for the presence of its subjects in those parts.' There were many who fervently believed in that goal, despite actions on the part of the conquerors, which did so much to defeat that purpose. The propriety of the way in which the conquest and colonization of the Indies was being carried out was called into question: doubts and disputes arose over the degree to which the

---

[21] Ruben C. Alvarado, "Vitoria's New World Order, The Great Commission and the Discovery of the New World", in *Contra Mundum*, No. 2 Winter 1992 [02_vitoria.pdf].

conquest of the Indies in fact exhibited a character exactly contrary to its avowed purpose. As Koenigsberger notes, 'It is to the great credit of the Spaniards that they debated these problems passionately and learnedly – no other European nation did, before the eighteenth century.'" [22]

Unlike the other European colonial powers of that age, the Spaniards were indeed vitally concerned with the moral problems of conquest, conversion, and government of the 'heathen peoples.' The debate reached its apex in the junta of Valladolid in 1550-1551, a public debate wanted by Charles V, between the Dominican Bartolomé de Las Casas and the theologian, Juan Ginés de Sepúlveda, whose details we'll see in the following chapter.

Spanish expansion in the Far East

The motivation of the Spanish expansion to the Far East was that the American possessions did not seem so advantageous as those under the Portuguese control for the spice-trade. When the Spaniards realized that Columbus and his successors had discovered neither Cathay nor the real Indies, they became concerned with finding a way around the Americas to the coveted Spice Islands of the Eastern seas.

The first Spanish expedition to the Far East in search of the Spicy Islands was led by Ferdinand Magellan (1480-1521, a Portuguese who had been in India in 1506, but later offered his service to Spain), in 1519-1521, who however reached only Cebu, in the central island of the Philippines, and met with a tragic death in the near Mactan island. A further expedition was led by Juan Garcia Jofre de Loaysa (1525), and a third one by Alvaro Saavedra (1527).

"With the appearance of the Spaniards in the Moluccas, the problem arose as to where the Atlantic line of demarcation set by the Tordesillas Treaty ran when continued on the other side of the globe. In fact, it followed approximately the meridian

---

[22] Ruben C. Alvarado, "Vitoria's New World Order… a.c. "In the words of Lewis Hanke: 'Probably never before, or since, has a mighty emperor… ordered his conquests to cease until it was decided if they were just.'

near where Tokyo in Japan and Adelaide in Australia are now situated, so that both the Moluccas and the Philippines were really on the Portuguese side of the line. But the sixteenth-century Spanish and Portuguese cosmographers had very different ideas about where the Tordesillas line ran when continued in the Eastern hemisphere. The Portuguese confidently claimed that the Moluccas were well within their sphere, whereas the Spaniards as obstinately maintained that not merely the Moluccas but China and even Malacca fell within the Spanish sphere. Clashes were therefore inevitable, and speedily occurred when the Spaniards attempted to follow up Magellan's voyage with similar expeditions. Portuguese opposition in the Moluccas proved too strong for such exhausted Spanish forces as survived the long Pacific crossing. In 1529 the Emperor Charles V recognized the strength of the Portuguese position by renouncing his claim to the Spice Islands in return for a cash indemnity in the Treaty of Zaragoza. "[23]

Consequently, Spain turned its main interest toward the Philippines islands. A fourth expedition left Mexico on 1st of November 1542, led by Ruy Lopez de Villalobos: he had received orders to colonize the 'Western Islands', which he renamed "Filipinas" in honor of Don Felipe, Prince of Asturias, the future Philip II. The expedition due to various causes did not succeed, and although it was ordered to keep clear from the Spice Islands, it reached Tidore in April 1544. After the imprisonment of the soldiers by the hands of the Portuguese and the death of Villalobos in 1546, assisted by the same St. Francis Xavier in Amboin, the Spanish fleet fell apart with some of the crew staying in the East and other returning to Europe on Portuguese boats.

Another expedition, led by Miguel Lopez de Legazpi (1502-1572), left Mexico on 21 November 1564 reaching Cebu on 27 April 1565, from where the conquest of the islands started.

In April 1571, Legazpi moved his headquarters to Luzon and occupied Manila without any difficulty, making it the final headquarters of the start of the conquest of Philippines. On his way to Luzon, Legazpi had ransomed fifty shipwrecked Chinese sailors from the Filipino tribesmen at Mindoro

---

[23] C.R. Boxer, *South-China in the Sixteenth Century* (Hakluyt Society 1953, Kraus Reprint Limited 1967), p. xxxvii-xxxviii. The Treaty of Zaragoza was a peace treaty signed on April 5, 1529, between King John II and the Emperor Charles V, which defined the areas of Spanish and Portuguese influence in the Far East.

and sent them back to China in one junk, in the hope of making a treaty of friendship with that country.

Spanish concern for China

The water around the Philippines continued to be the scene of operations by merchants. Chinese merchants from Fujian had been trading intermittently with the Philippines Islands for centuries. Rumors about the wealth of the China trade tickled the ears of the Spaniards, also out of envy for the Portuguese profitable trade. There were two possible ways: gaining a foothold in a port of China, as the Portuguese have done, or trying the military conquest of the country. Legazpi and his successors followed the first way, but the second way, also, as we will see later in details, was not fully discarded. Legazpi died in August 1572 and was succeeded by Guido de Lavezares, the royal treasurer of the expedition (from 1572 to 1575).

The coasts were also frequented by pirates. In the early years of 1570, a Chinese pirate, named Limahon or Lin Feng, started his damaging operations from the coasts of China down to the Philippines. In November 1574 with its large fleet, he approached Manila. The Spanish soldiers could stand his two attacks, forcing him to withdraw further north on Pangasinan coast. There, he was blockaded by Juan de Salcedo, who even succeeded to burn the fleet of the pirate. Meanwhile, the Chinese imperial authorities sent an officer, named Omolon (Wang Wanggao), in search of the pirate. He was well received by the governor Lavezares and could establish a friendly acquaintance with the Spaniards. Satisfied about the conditions of the pirate and with the promise that he would be handed to China dead or alive, he decided to go back, and, in return for the favors at their hands, agreed to convey to China a Spanish delegation. For this mission in 1575, two Augustinian friars were selected, Fray Martin de Herrada (or Rada) and Fray Jeronimo Marin, with two soldiers as an escort, Pedro Sarmiento and Miguel de Loarca. The objectives were to assure China of the friendship of Spain, to get the permit for the missionaries to freely preach the Gospel and to obtain a trading spot, as the Portuguese had in Macao, as well as to collect as much documentation as possible on the economic and social situation of the country as well as on the character, custom and traditions of people. As we will see more in detail the development of the embassy, it could not achieve any of its objectives, mainly because the pirate Lin Feng managed to escape the blockade, return to the Chinese coasts and continued his adventures.

Despite the failure of the first embassy, a number of people continued to urge the importance and the convenience of sending an embassy to China.

"One the acts of Governor Dr. Francisco de Sande [from 1575 to 1580] was to send Father Jeronimo Marin to Spain to inform the king about affairs in the Philippines. The priest, very much interested in the conversion of China, informed the king, either on instructions of the governor or on his own initiative, about what he had observed in there. This prompted Philip II around 1581 to dispatch an embassy to the empire, naming as ambassadors Fathers Marin, Francisco de Ortega who later was the bishop of Nueva Caceres, and Juan Gonzales de Mendoza, much later bishop of Lipari and Chiapa successively. But the whole mission was dissolved, despite the good will of the king, because Father Gonzales de Mendoza did not proceed from Mexico and the Audencia of this city, commissioned for the purpose by the king, judged insufficient the gifts which they were bringing from Madrid to the emperor of China." [24]

Mendoza and Ortega left Spain in February 1582 for Mexico, with a letter dated on June 5, 1581 of King Philip II to Wanli Emperor of China. The Viceroy of Mexico, Conde de Coruna, first very keen about the embassy, changed his mind. It was decided to wait for the arrival of the returning governor of the Philippines Francisco de Sande, who, however, considered the project useless. The Viceroy referred the matter to the king who cancelled the embassy.

Bu in Manila, the union of the Spain and Portugal into the hands of King Philip in 1581, provided an occasion for another embassy. The death

---

[24] Augustinian Juan Gonzalez de Mendoza, "Historia del Gran Reyno de China (Madrid, Pedro Madrigal Printer, 1586) in I Part (3 books) and II Part (2 books): it includes the writings of Galeote Pereira, a seaman who experienced Chinese prisons, of the Dominican friar Gaspar da Cruz O.P. and Augustinian Martin de Rada O.S.A., as well as the Itinerary of Franciscan Friars, who had visited China. The book became very popular: it was translated into numerous languages. It is held to be the first book printed in Europe that reproduced the characters of Chinese writing.

of the Cardinal-King of Portugal in January 1580 [25] was followed by a dynastical crisis, with three grandchildren of Manuel I, claiming the throne: Catherine, Duchess of Braganza, Antonio, Prior of Crato, and Philip II of Spain. António was acclaimed King of Portugal by the people of Santarem on July 1580, and then in other cities and towns throughout the country. But members of the Council of Governors of Portugal, who supported Philip, escaped to Spain and declared him to be the legal successor of Henry. Philip II marched into Portugal and defeated the troops loyal to the Prior of Crato and arrived to Lisbon. Philip II of Spain was crowned Philip I of Portugal in 1581. It was a personal dynasty: Philip promises to preserve Portuguese autonomy, merging the crowns rather than the kingdoms.

On March 14, 1582, as soon as the news of the union arrived in Manila, the Spanish Governor Gonzalo Ronquillo de Penalosa (from April 1580 to March 10, 1583) sent the Jesuit Fr. Alonso Sanchez to Macau as his ambassador to solicit the acceptance of Philip II as king of both Spain and Portugal, and to try to obtain a trading port from the Chinese authorities. After some misadventure in China, Sanchez reached Macau at the end of May. He broke the news of the union to the highest authorities, showing the official dispatches. They promised to recognize the union but they wanted a confirmation from the Viceroy in Goa. Sanchez left Macau on July 6 back to Manila via Japan, feeling to have accomplished his mission.[26] Unfortunately, he had to return to Macau on November 3, after a shipwreck in Taiwan. It was only on December 18, that the Portuguese in Macau rather reluctantly made their official oath of allegiance acknowledging the union of the two countries (until 31 May 1642).

In 1584-1585 there was another mission of Fr. Alfonso Sanchez and the *Real Fator* (Royal Factor) Juan Batista Roman, sent by the acting governor

---

[25] In Portugal, King Manuel reigned from 1495 to 1521: it was the golden era of Portugal, setting up its colonial empire. Juan III, his son, reigned from 1521 to 1554, starting the decline as a political and commercial power. The king Sebastian I of Portugal reigned from 1554 to 1578. At his killing during an expedition against Morocco, he was succeeded by the son of Manuel, Henry, the Cardinal-King until his death in January 1580.

[26] José S. Arcilla, in "Alonso Sanchez: Jesuit Diplomat to the Portuguese in Macao" (A.N. Baxter at alii, eds., *Conference Proceedings of Macao-Philippines Historical Relations*, Macao: Universidade de Macao & CESEPA, 2005, pp. 156-176) gives high praise to Sanchez's diplomatic ability and tact, but it seems without substantial justification, especially as far as his relationship with Fr. Valignano is concerned.

Diego Ronquillo (from March 1583 to May 1584) to Macau, in order to set into order the mutiny of the crew of the galleon St. Juan and at the same time to solicit from the Chinese authorities the sending of an official Spanish embassy to Beijing. It met with failure.

In 1593, another embassy left Manila, composed of Don Francisco de Castro and the Dominican Fathers Luis Gandullo and Juan de Castro, heading for Fujian, in search of the assassins of governor Dom Gomez Perez Dasmariñas (from 1590 to 1593), who had been killed in 25 October 1593 by some Chinese seamen off the coast of Batangas, on his way to conquer Moluccas. Unfortunately, the embassy accomplished nothing.

Early in 1598, Captain Joan Çamudio (Juan de Zamudio) sailed for China, to purchase iron, saltpeter, lead, tin, and other very necessary articles for the provision of the camp at Manila. He encountered resistance to his entry in China on the part of the Portuguese from Macao, who wanted to prevent the Spanish from sharing the trade with China. But the Canton authorities not only did not believe the calumnies against the Spaniards, but even assigned to the Spaniards a port 8 or 12 leagues from Canton, called Pinal (Pine Grove), where they could go there freely to trade and for any other purpose. They were allowed to buy a house inside the city of Canton, where they could stay by night. No longer after Joan Zamudio entered in this harbor, he was informed that Luis Perez Dasmariñas, on his trip to Cambodia, ran into a storm and had landed just South of Macau. After a while, Dasmariñas arrived at Pinal with his men and the remains of the shipwreck, on vessels given them by the Chinese, avoiding the Portuguese of Macau. He, willing to continue his Cambodia expedition, immediately went to Canton to ask permission to buy a new ship. Joan de Çamudio helped to accommodate it with some artillery. Then, towards the end of December 1598, however, he set sail from Pinal, leaving Dasmariñas and his men settled there, waiting for permission to leave China with their ship. In a few days. Çamudio reached the coast of Luzon in safety, bringing Dasmariñas' request of help. The governor Francisco Tello (from 1596 to May 1692) immediately sent the required things on a vessel, which was about to sail to the kingdom of Siam, led by Captain Joan de Mendoza y Gamboa. A little later, in the month of May, some trading ships came from China to Manila, bringing letters from Dasmariñas, with news about the preparations for his expedition and about the persecutions he suffered from the Portuguese of Macau. In the middle of June 1599, four soldiers were sent by

Dasmariñas to Manila to inform Francisco Tello, that he was still at Pinal in distress. He had bought a Chinese ship at Canton, which seemed in good condition, in order to continue his voyage to Cambodia. Having embarked, he was already two days on his way, when the ship began to leak, so that due to this danger, he was obliged to return to Pinal. He asked the governor to send him assistance in men, arms, and munitions, and also a ship, in order to continue his voyage. The governor advised him to return to Manila and abandon the enterprise. The message was sent through Captain Joan Tello, who soon left for Pinal, to continue the good beginning made by Joan de Çamudio. However, the Spanish presence in Pinal did not last long.[27]

The Spaniards had to wait the XVII century to restart contacts with Formosa (Taiwan), with the establishment of a military post on the island around 1625-26. But even then, only for few years.

---

[27] Antonio de Morga, *History of the Philippines Islands*, in http://www.gutenberg.org/etext/7001.

2

EVANGELIZATION OF THE NEW WORLD THROUGH THE 'PATRONAGE SYSTEM' OF THE KINGDOMS OF SPAIN AND PORTUGAL

The Religious Context

The atmosphere within the Catholic Church in the XVI century was, at first, rather pessimistic due to several factors: the wavering of the faith and of charitable services of many Catholics, the sweeping reform launched by Martin Luther in October 1517 in Germany, together with the danger of Conciliarism, that is the view that a general council of the Church has greater authority than the Pope, which was paralyzing a lot of the work of the Holy See. Soon a strong need for a reaction was felt. Great impulses of the Catholic Counter-Reformation arose from the foundation of new religious orders and congregations, especially the Society of Jesus founded in 1534 through the initiative of St. Ignatius Loyola (1491-1556). The new religious bodies pioneered a Catholic revival.

The 'Lutheran Protest' was a shock, but probably, what really forced the Roman Curia into thoughts of reform was the Sack of Rome in 1527 by mutinous imperial troops. Even lax curia bureaucrats interpreted it as a judgment of God on the abuses and confusion, which had too long been tolerated in papal and episcopal administration.

Paul III (r. 1534-49) succeeded in breaking through the heavy weight of traditions and customs. During his pontificate he sponsored a commission, which during the years 1536-37 studied the causes of the Catholic crisis that had provoked the Protestant Reform. The commission frankly pointed out the abuses. Paul III, then, set up a standing committee to decide and follow up the reform of these abuses, thus gradually creating a completely reorganized papal curia. And, to defy Conciliarism, he summoned the Council of Trent (1545-1563), which clarified the Catholic doctrine in response to the Protestant challenges and provided guidelines for the Christian life.

However, all the concerns for the affairs within the Church did not force the majority of the Popes, during the XVI century, to neglect the problem outside the Church, mainly the evangelization of the new peoples, whose existence the geographical discoveries were gradually revealing. Popes, as the heads of the Church, needed to evolve a new system and method for hastening the evangelization of these territories: consequently, they adopted the 'Patronage System', and granted a combination of rights, privileges, and duties to the Crowns of Portugal and Spain as patrons of and responsible for the Catholic Missions and ecclesiastical establishments in the "New World," namely Africa, Asia and Latin America.

The exercise of the *Real Padroado / Patronato Real* and the close cooperation between the Church and the State in the promotion of Christian missionary activity was based upon the doctrinal position of the Papacy, which then was vigorously upheld, that is, *'temporal possessions were occupied unlawfully by the infidels in the new conquered lands' and that these lands 'should be allotted among the faithful.'* Due to his supreme religious authority, the Pope was considered also the ruler of the world, and, consequently, it was a common belief that all the newly discovered lands belonged to him and to the kings to whom he granted the right of possession. The local population of these regions were generally considered 'uncivilized', at times, even 'less than human', and, consequently, considered as 'deprived of any right'.

Royal Patronage of Portugal

Towards the end of the XV century, the dominant Christian nations of Portugal and Spain were successfully engaged in explorations and discoveries of new lands. The Popes favored Portugal first, as we have seen, from the approval of the Order of the Knights of Christ by Pope John XXII's Bull *Ad ea ex quibus cultus* (14 March 1319) and the appointment of Prince Henry the Navigator (1394-1460) as its Prior in 1420. Together with other papal documents, they marked the foundation of Portugal's ecclesiastical jurisdiction in the conquered territories, the Portuguese patronage upon the Catholic missions. Later, the Popes started to favor also Spain in its discoveries. It seemed appropriate to require from both kingdoms greater efforts to propagate the faith in the newly discovered regions. Thus developed the *padroado system.*

The objectives of the Papacy to favor the Portuguese conquests in Africa were threefold: to contact the legendary Christian kingdom of the 'Prester

John', to stop the pirate attacks from the 'Moors' (or Muslim) on the Mediterranean coasts and the evangelization of the new peoples. When in 1415, the Portuguese expedition, sent by King John I, conquered Ceuta in Morocco, Pope Martin V erected the diocese of Ceuta, and asked the assistance of the Portuguese Crown to further the propagation of faith.

Meanwhile, on June 18, 1452, Pope Nicholas V with the Bull *Dum Diversas*, and on January 8, 1454, with the Bull *Romanus Pontifex*, entrusted to King Alphonse V of Portugal and Prince Henry, as we have seen, the duty to foster the evangelization work, the foundation and the administration of the Church in the new lands: … *in the provinces, islands, and places already acquired, and to be acquired by him, may found and cause to be founded and built any churches, monasteries, or other pious places whatsoever; and also may send over to them any ecclesiastical persons whatsoever, as volunteers, both seculars, and regulars of any of the mendicant orders (with license, however, from their superiors), and that those persons may abide there as long as they shall live, and hear confessions of all who live in the said parts or who come thither…*

In 1456, Pope Callixtus III entrusted to Prince Henry, the Prior or Master of the Order of the Knights of Christ, the power of spiritual supervision over all the existing and future dominions of the Crown of Portugal. After the death of Prince Henry in 1460, the mastership of the Order was held by the royal family of Portugal. Thus, started the change of the Order from a religious congregation of soldier-monks to a more political institution, with the *padroado* falling into political hands.

In 1514, Pope Leo X established the diocese of Funchal on Madeira Island, off the African coast.[28] India and Brazil were attached to it, and the Portuguese king was given the patronage of this enormous diocese. The king was also made the administrator of the Order of Christ, with all the authorities over the diocese.

Padroado took effect in India and in Asia in 1533, when Pope Paul III set up Goa as a suffragan diocese of Funchal Archdiocese. The document that founded Goa also gave a concrete explanation of the term. According

---

[28] The Diocese of Funchal was created on January 12, 1514, through the Bull *Pro excellenti præeminentia* of Pope Leo X, following the elevation of Funchal from Village to the status of Town by King Manuel I of Portugal (from August 21, 1508). The new diocese was suffragan of the Archdiocese of Lisbon.

to it, the king was authorized to propose candidate for bishopric and certain other offices in the diocese, but it was his responsibility to fund it: he should pay for all Church offices and their maintenance. He should also fund the construction of new monasteries, chapels and churches and repair the old ones. Besides, he should also provide for the necessary articles for divine worship.

The conviction that Portugal was the missionary nation above all the others in the West, *Alferes da Fe*, standard bearers of Faith, was widespread and deeply rooted among people. Royal dispatches emphasized the first and principal obligation of the Kings of Portugal "to forward the work of conversion by all means in their power."

Development between Portugal and Spain

After the arrival of Christopher Columbus to Hispaniola in 1492, the king of Spain also was invested by Pope Alexander VI with full rights of 'royal patronage' (*patronato real*) over all the churches of the "Indies," placing all religious affairs under the control of the Council of Indies. Soon, competition between Spain and Portugal flared up.

In May 1493, Pope Alexander VI tried to mediate between the two powers: he set forth three Bulls, in which the controversy could be definitely settled by dividing the area of control. With the Bull *Inter Coetera* (4 May 1493), he recognized the exclusive right of the Spanish crown to trade with land that had been or might be discovered to the west of the Atlantic Ocean, and at the same time laid on the king the injunction to bring Christian faith to peoples in those lands.

In another Bull, *Piis Fidelium,* in June 1493, Alexander VI granted Spain the vicarial power to propose bishops and send missionaries to the 'Indies'.

Consequently, both kingdoms of Portugal and Spain started their expansion and conquest of the "New World," taking with them also Catholic missionaries for the evangelization of the new peoples. The Bull of July 4, 1508, *Universalis Ecclesiæ Regimini* of Julius II gives the details of these privileges: no churches, monasteries, or religious foundations could be erected, in territory already discovered or to be subsequently discovered, without the consent of the kings. It conferred also on them the power of proposing suitable candidates for any metropolitan and other sees. Bishops were obliged to confer canonical institution to ecclesiastical beneficiaries ten days after the royal notification had been made. It also conferred the right to present candidates for all the abbacies and prelacies of the regulars and, indeed, for every ecclesiastical benefice, large or small. The kings also had the right of designating the boundaries of all new dioceses, of sending religious personnel to the Indies, of determining their stay there and their transfer from one province to another. Religious establishments were under the supervision of the Council of the Indies, through a commissioner. The provincial or custodian of the regular clergy was named by their general, but he had to be notified to the commissioner, who communicated with the Council of the Indies, and without its permission the nomination should be suspended.

During the XVI century, Portugal was so successful in the enterprise that it seemed to provide a satisfactory guarantee of the permanence of the policy. The Papacy, having skillfully divested itself of financial responsibility for these distant missions, may have felt well pleased with it. However, bad effects of the system, with abuses and disorders, were increasing day by day. Strong debates rose about the suitability of the patronage rights, first, concerning the rights and methods for the conquest of the new lands and, later, about the system itself.

Debate on the Colonial Conquest

The royal patronage of the Iberian monarchs constituted an absolute system of control, based upon "the donation of the Holy Apostolic See and other legitimate titles" to them with the main objective of the evangelization of the "New World." Queen Isabella declared, at the very beginning of the conquest, that *"Castille possessed a just title to the Indies because of its obligation to evangelize the Indians, and, indeed, this was the sole justification for the presence of its subjects in those parts."* [29]

---

[29] Quoted in Ruben C. ALVARADO, "Vitoria's New World Order: The Great Commission and the Discovery of the New World", in *Contra Mundum*, No. 2, Winter 1992 (http://www.contra-mundum.org/cm/features/02_vitoria.pdf).

In the mentioned papal Bulls to the kings of Portugal and Spain, the attitude of Popes was founded upon a then popular doctrine: starting from the primacy of the supernatural objective of the salvation of souls, the conclusion was that Popes had full authority on the entire Christian community and on the whole world. In virtue of the divine and papal commands, the Gospel had to be brought to all peoples by the Christian States, and this could not be done without the employment of physical power and political means. So, the Pope could entrust the new lands to the kings of Spain and Portugal together with the duty of preaching the Gospel and of the administration of the Missions.

Several authors not only have sought to prove the thesis that the conversion of the pagan races necessitated their political conquest and subjection, with the employment of physical power and military means, but also, based on renowned medieval authorities, quoting particularly Aristotle, the Indians were considered as irrational beings, whose inherently inferior condition immediately made them slaves by nature. So, if they refused to accept the European rule, they could be enslaved. Furthermore, if the Indians resisted enslavement, the European had the legitimate right to wage war on them. Upon these principles, the Spaniards launched the *"encomienda"* system, a system whereby 'Indian' workers were allocated to Spanish settlers as slaves, on the understanding that they would be instructed in the Christian faith in return for their labor.

> *"The papal demarcation* [of the world] *and title of patronage, which inseparably linked the propagation of the Christian faith with the discoveries as their central idea and chief object, were recognized not only by the two kingdoms concerned and other states, but were expressly invoked by the contemporary literature - juridical, theological and missiological - to justify the subjection of the pagan races in so far as these would not receive the missionaries or persisted in interfering with their work."[30]*

Out of such a situation, the theological issues were raised about several aspects: the moral justification of the conquest by war of the new lands, the deprivation of the indigenous people of their properties and their liberty,

---

[30] H. de la COSTA, *The Jesuits in the Philippines* (Cambridge, Mass.: Harvard University Press, 1967) pp. 37-57. 77-106. See also Joseph SCHMIDLIN, *Catholic Mission History* (Techny, Ill.: Mission Press SVD, 1933), pp. 263-264.

40

as well as the judgment of the local people as inferior or irrational human beings. The debate on these issues was later extended to its foundations: the relationship between law and gospel, church and state, the doctrine of the just war, etc., thus, starting the formation of a new field of research, which is the study of the global and international relations. It turned out to be an important intellectual controversy. However, although the debate and the disagreement were evident, unfortunately, the *conquistadores* of both Spain and Portugal continued in their pursuit of violent conquest and of employing brutal methods.

One of the first to challenge such a behavior and mentality was Fr. Antonio de Montesinos, one of the first Dominicans to arrive in the island of Hispaniola, where he saw the serious abuses and ill-treatments the Spanish *conquistadores* reserved to the natives. In a sermon on Christmas Day 1511, he dared to challenge their behavior:

"I am the voice crying in the wilderness... the voice of Christ in the desert of this island... You are all in mortal sin... on account of the cruelty and tyranny with which you treat these innocent people. Are these not men? Have they not rational souls? Must not you love them as you love yourselves?"

Only a year after the sermon by Montesinos, condemning his compatriots' brutal treatment of the Caribbean Indians, the Spanish monarchs issued a series of laws intended to regulate Indian-Spaniard relations, the Burgos Laws (27 December 1512, with Amendments in the following July). They constituted the first systematic code to govern the conduct of settlers in America, particularly in their relations with the native people. Among other innovations, the Laws initiated the official use of the old Spanish legal term *encomienda*, with its implication of duties and privileges, mainly the instruction in the Christian faith of the local subjects. [31]

The provisions in the Laws for the protection of the natives were considered by the missionaries to be inadequate; but they represented the first small breach in the wall of official indifference. However, although new, the Laws soon fell into oblivion by the *encomenderos*. But, the opposition to their behavior and methods continued mainly by the initiatives of the

---

[31] For the quotation and information see
http://faculty.smu.edu/bakewell/BAKEWELL/texts/burgoslaws.html.

missionaries, among whom the most prominent were the Dominican friars, Bartolomé de Las Casas (1484-1566) and Francisco de Victoria (1485-1546).

Bartolomé de Las Casas [32] strongly contributed to keep up the opposition. In 1502, he, as a young man, went to see his family's possessions on Hispaniola. By then, the natives of the island had been mostly subdued as slaves. Las Casas accompanied the Governor on two different military missions aimed at pacifying the natives who remained on the island. On one of these, the young man witnessed a massacre of poorly-armed natives. He traveled around the island a great deal, and was able to see the deplorable conditions in which the natives were kept. Over the next few years, Las Casas traveled to Spain and back several times, finishing his theological studies and being ordained priest. By 1514, he decided that he could no longer be personally involved in the exploitation of the natives, and renounced his family holdings on Hispaniola. He became convinced that the enslavement and slaughter of the native population was a mortal sin and an awful crime.

During his returns to Spain, he looked for support to establish new towns in which Spaniard and Indian would live together in peace and equality, but without great success due to the opposition of the *encomenderos*. Disappointed with the results of his political activities, in 1523, Las Casas joined the Dominicans in Santo Domingo and focused his energy on writing. Over the next several years he wrote several works including the treatise *Concerning the Only Way of Drawing All Peoples to the True Religion* and the beginnings of both *Apologetica historia de las Indias* and *Historia de las Indies*.

Meanwhile, from 1526 on, another Dominican, Fr. Francisco de Vitoria was appointed to the Prime Chair of theology at the University of Salamanca. It was the custom at the time for professors at the end of each year to give a *relectio* or review of an important matter of doctrine. Vitoria gave many of these in his twenty-year-long career there, of which fourteen have been preserved. The *relectiones, De Indiis* [Of the Indies] and *De Jure belli Hispanorum in barbaros,* [Of the right of war of the Spaniards upon the

---

[32] Bartolomé de Las Casas: from Colonist to Defender of the Indians; http://oregonstate.edu/instruct/phl302/philosophers/las_casas.html; http://elvis.rowan.edu/~kilroy/jek/07/17.html.

42

barbarians], summarized his ideas and were seminal to the future development of the field.[33]

The controversy as he saw it consisted in three questions: by what right are the Indian nations subjected to the Spaniards; what power do the princes of the Spaniards have over the Indian nations with respect to temporal and civil matters; what power do both these princes and the Church have over the Indian nations with respect to spiritual things and religion.

Francisco de Vitoria's position did not follow an extreme view: he denied the right of conquest on the basis of the papal concession of land to the Kings, or their pretension to universal rule as the Roman Empire, or on the status of the Indians as sinners, pagans, or irrational creatures, but he justified indirectly the occupation of the colonies by the necessity of the evangelization when obstructed, and of the protection of the missionaries and of the local faithful if persecuted.

The *junta* of Valladolid, 1550-1551

In 1537, Paul III with Bull *Sublimis Deus*, took part to the debate proclaiming the Indians' capability to understand and receive the Christian faith since they were rational beings.

"We... consider, however, that the Indians are truly men and that they are not only capable of understanding the Catholic Faith but, according to our information, they desire exceedingly to receive it. Desiring to provide ample remedy for these evils, We define and declare by these Our letters... that the said Indians and all other people who may later be discovered by Christians, are by no means to be deprived of their liberty or the possession of their property, even though they be outside the faith of Jesus Christ; and that they may and should, freely and legitimately, enjoy their liberty and the possession of their property; nor should they be in any way enslaved; should the contrary happen, it shall be null and have no effect."

---

[33] On the position of Vitoria, here are summarized the arguments given in Ruben C. ALVARADO, "Vitoria's New World Order: The Great Commission and the Discovery of the New World", in *Contra Mundum*, No. 2, Winter 1992 (http://www.contramundum.org/cm/features/02_vitoria.pdf).

In the same year, Fr. Las Casas tried again to show that natives could be controlled peacefully and that violence and conquest were unnecessary. He was able to convince the crown to let him send missionaries to a region in north-central Guatemala where the natives had proved particularly fierce. His experiment worked, and the natives were brought under Spanish control peacefully. The experiment was called *Vera Paz*, or "true peace," and the region still bears the name. Unfortunately, once the region was brought under control, greedy colonists took the lands and enslaved the natives, undoing almost all of Las Casas' work.

In 1540, Las Casas returned to Spain to lobby for new legislation to protect the natives. Charles V was sympathetic, and passed the New Laws of 1542. These laws limited the corrupt *encomienda* system, prohibiting Indian slavery and safeguarding the rights of the Indians. The "New Laws of the Indies for the Good Treatment and Preservation of the Indians" (November 20, 1542) consisted of many regulations on the *encomienda* system, including the solemn prohibition of the enslavement of the Indians and provisions for the gradual abolition of the *encomienda* system. They stated that the natives would be considered free persons, and the *encomenderos* could no longer demand their labor. The natives would be paid wages in exchange for their labor. The *encomienda* grants would not be hereditary.

The first Viceroy of Peru tried to enforce the New Laws which caused the *encomenderos* to revolt in a large-scale bloody rebellion. Having seen this, the Viceroy of New Spain decided not to enforce the New Laws in his territories. In this way due to massive pressure from the *encomenderos* the New Laws were never implemented in the two largest colonies of the Spanish Empire. Finally, in 1545, the rule stating that the *encomienda* system would no longer be hereditary was revoked, and the place of the *encomienda* system was again secure. Although the New Laws were largely unsuccessful, they did result in the liberation of thousands of indigenous workers.

In 1544, Las Casas was made Bishop of Chiapas in Guatemala, and returned to the Americas to implement the new laws, but he met considerable resistance. He himself was in danger of being killed for his role in enforcing them. Back to Spain in 1547, he gave up the episcopal ministry, and devoted the rest of his life to speaking and writing on behalf of the Indians.

In this background, he found himself at the center of an academic debate. The secular scholar Juan Ginés de Sepúlveda had written a treatise, which defended the conquest as necessary. Using Aristotle's theory of natural slavery, Sepúlveda declared that the Spanish had a moral duty to assert control over the natives of the new lands. Las Casas refuted Sepúlveda's claims, and a series of debates took place in Valladolid in 1550-1551 in a public debate in front of a *junta*, of a group of jurists and theologians, ordered by the King of Spain, Charles V.

The debate, however, was carried out in a strictly theoretical manner, exclusively relying on European secular and religious sources. Although Las Casas tried to prove his thesis with his experiences while he lived in the New World, both he and Sepúlveda failed to compromise.

The *junta* did not reach any clear-cut decision regarding the justification of the conquest and its relationship with the propagation of the Christian faith to the Indians. On one hand, the jurists and theologians of Valladolid could not have conceivably recommended to Charles V to permanently stop all wars of conquest in the New World and to merely seek the peaceful Christianization of the Indians, as Las Casas had proposed. On the other hand, if Sepúlveda's harsh attack on Indian culture was intended to influence the Spanish crown to revoke the 1542 New Laws, he failed, for Las Casas effectively frustrated any immediate attempts by the *encomenderos* to have the laws revoked.

In the ensuing years after Valladolid, Sepúlveda continued to be the champion of the *encomenderos*, while Las Casas established himself as the outstanding defender of the Indians. He continued working on his monumental history, *Historia de las Indias*. In 1552, he published a very short version of it entitled *A Brief Report of the Destruction of the Indies* (or *Tears of the Indians*), which caused quite a stir and gained him a lot of support for his cause in Spain.

"Colonial Policy: unlike the other European colonists of that age, the Spaniards were vitally concerned with the moral problems of conquest, conversion, and government of heathen peoples. If the great majority of conquistadores ruthlessly pursued gold, power, and status, they took with them Dominican and Franciscan friars who set themselves to convert and educate the American Indians and, sometimes, to protect them from the Spanish masters. The Dominican Bartolomé de Las Casas fought long battles to modify at least the greatest evils of colonial exploitation. His debates with a theologian, Juan Ginés de Sepulveda, and the writings of Francisco de Vitoria provide the first systematic discussions of the moral and legal problems of conquest and colonial rule. Their importance lay in their effects on Spanish colonial

legislation. The Leyes Nuevas *(New Laws of the Indies) of 1542 were based largely on the arguments of Las Casas. While in the colonies these laws were honored more in the breach than in the observance, yet they provided at least some protection for the Indians, and there was nothing like them in any of the other European overseas colonies of the period..."* [34]

The Debate in the Philippines

Outside Spain and Spanish America, the above debated issues also had some impact. First, with the conquest of the Philippines in 1571, Spaniards once again faced the issue of Spain's right of conquest.

The Spaniards went to the Philippines and started their conquest feeling fully justified for their war and the adopted methods, based upon the motivation of the evangelization of the natives, according to the predominant mentality. The first point of conflict, also in the Philippines, was the ill-treatment of the natives by the hands of the Spanish authorities. The first bishop of Manila, the Dominican Domingo Salazar was appalled by the corrupt and venal practices pervading in Manila, when he arrived at the end of 1581. As in Mexico, he deplored all the abuses against the natives carried out by the Spaniards, their bad morals, vulgarities and blasphemies. In a letter dated 20 June 1582, he appealed to King Philip II to redress the local people's sufferings and in Manila he summoned a Synod to discuss the issue.

"The underlying issue faced by the Manila Synod was the role of Spain in the Philippines. The fathers accepted the de facto Spanish occupation of the islands. They pointed out, however, that it was justifiable neither by inheritance or donation, nor by just war, but only by the papal delegation to spread the Christian Gospel, in exchange for which the Spanish crown could discover and rule the new world. Neither the royal officials nor the soldiers had any title to the islands except what the king had granted them. And the king has granted them only as much power as he had received, namely, the faculty to send preachers of the Gospel throughout the world, but not to dispossess anyone of what belonged to him. The royal personage might also send others to protect the ministers of the Gospel and their new converts, and they could impose temporal government over the latter in order to facilitate

---

[34] Enciclopedia Britannica (Macropedia), *Spain, History of,* (William Benton Publisher 1943-1973), vol. 17, p. 424

their conversion and confirmation in the new faith. But it did not follow that 'they may, as they have already done, appropriate everything to themselves, for the Gospel does not deprive anyone of what belongs to him.' And in lands where there were no obstacles to the spread of the faith, where people were capable by themselves of leading a supernatural life, and where there were guarantees that the Gospel would be preached – in these lands it would be an act of tyranny to overthrow the native government. For the Gospel deprives no one of what he has; rather 'it supplies what one did not have, preserves and perfects what he already has'...
Hence, the Synod, concluded, it was imperative not only to send ministers of the Gospel, but also to provide everything for the spiritual up-lifting of the native population. For the sake of the Gospel, then, the Spaniards could govern the islands, dispatch cedulas, laws, just and truly Christian ordinances...'" [35]

So, in the Philippines, the war of conquest was generally considered justified by the need of the evangelization of people, although the methods were condemned.

The ongoing debate in Europe

The theoretical debate continued in Europe, but with the main emphasis on the legitimacy of the colonial enterprise.

Juan de Solorzano Pereira (1575-1655) studied jurisprudence in Salamanca and in 1609 was appointed judge in the *Audiencia* of Lima, a position that he held until 1627. He wrote a number of books on legal matters, but his most important was *De Indiorum jure disputatione* (Madrid, 1629), which he subsequently adapted and translated into Spanish, with the title *Politica Indiana*. The book describes the discovery of the Indies and discusses the legality of the conquest and of Spanish occupation. He enumerated ten titles of possession: God's will, discovery with divine help, *ius primi occupantis* (right of the first occupier), the barbarism and uncivilized state of the Indians, their unbelief, their unnatural crimes, the necessity of their conversion, their obligation to receive missionaries, the pontifical and the

---

[35] José S. ARCILLA, "Christian Missions to China and the Philippines", in *Philippine Studies*, vol. 31, 4th Quarter 1983, pp. 469-470, quoting the "Actas del Primer Sinodo de Manila (1582-86), Libro 1, Cap. 1, *Philippiniana Sacra* [1969]: 435-38).

imperial commission. He pointed out that even England and France recognized the papal decree of demarcation. In the remainder of the *Politica,* Solorzano addressed various themes such as Indian freedom, the *encomienda* system, the ecclesiastical affairs, the Royal Patronage, the secular government and the economy of the Indies. His book systematizes law and politics in colonial America: it is a fundamental text concerning Spain's imperial politics.

The Spanish government, which at that time controlled also Portugal, adopted the work of Solorzano as a guide to its rights and responsibilities in India. Naturally, Rome had no hesitation in placing on the Index of Prohibited Books the section of the work, which dealt with ecclesiastical affairs (20 March 1642).

The Jesuit Fr. Josè Acosta (1540-1600) proposed a middle course: he upheld, on one hand, that the unbelievers must never be coerced into conversion, but on the other hand, he held that a purely apostolic procedure of peaceful methods was impossible under the existing circumstances; consequently, the missionaries were to follow the apostolic methods in so far as possible, but whenever necessary, they needed to have the protection of the civil power (*De procuranda Indorum salute,* II).

The debate went on dealing with the Patronage system itself: it was based upon the two interpretations of its meaning, being either a Privilege which could be modified by the Holy See, or a Right for Spain and Portugal, that should not be interfered even by Rome. This debate brought to the decision of Pope Gregory XV (1554-1623, r. since 1621) to establish the Sacred Congregation for the Evangelization of Peoples (or Propaganda Fide, SCPF) on January 6, 1622, which represented not only a result of the reform programs, proposed by the Council of Trent. More pointedly, but also a late admission that to have put missionary activities under the control of Portugal and Spain had not been a wise and effective solution. Without trying to denigrate previous sacrifices made by the two kingdoms and by hosts of earlier missionaries, the Holy See felt the need for a more direct reform and supervision. Consequently, Rome started to establish Apostolic Vicariates outside the control of Portuguese and Spanish governments, both in Asia (India and China, in particular) and in Latin America. Their heads and personnel were chosen and appointed by the Holy See.

However, the governments of both Spain and Portugal opposed the new system and continued to reclaim their 'rights'. In 1681, Spain published the *Recopilacion de Leyes de lor Reynos de las Indias (Collection of the Laws of the Kingdoms of the Indies)*. It was the Crown's response to the great debates of the XVI century over the juridical status of the Indians, the justice of the conquest, and the distribution of *encomiendas*. The *Recopilacion* opened with the high-sounding affirmation that the *'Lord God had given the King the possession of the newly discovered land across the ocean-sea'* and that, consequently, the King was 'more obliged than any other prince in the world' to promote the entry of the native people of the Indies into the flock of the Holy Roman Catholic Church. In basing royal authority on the mandate of Heaven, the Laws of the Indies echoed the previous Spanish absolutist tradition. The object of the *Recopilacion* intended thus not merely to provide an indispensable instrument of government for magistrates and courts, but also to demonstrate the justice and legitimacy of Spanish rule in the New World.[36]

The Patronage System continued, creating further problems. In the XIX and XX centuries these patronage privileges were sought by other countries. The conflicts continued up to 1926 when the Holy See abolished the whole system.[37]

Missionary efforts of Portugal and Spain

In 1497, Vasco de Gama (ca.1460-1524) left Lisboa for the Indies, accompanied by two Trinitarian priests, one of whom died on the trip but the other, Pedro de Covilham, landed in Calicut in 1498. On his voyage in 1500 to Brazil and to India, Pedro Alvares Cabral (1467-1520) had with him a vicar, eight secular clergymen and eight Franciscans. On his voyage in 1503, Alfonso de Alburquerque (1453-1515) had five Dominicans under

---

[36] For further details, see D. A. Brading, *The First America: The Spanish Monarchy, Creole Patriots, and the Liberal State 1492-1867* (Cambridge University Press, 1991: available in H:\ChurchCHINA\StoriaXVsecCina\The First America the Spanish - Google Book Search.mht).

[37] For further details of the history of the 'Patronage system' in China, see Sergio Ticozzi, "Ending Civil Patronage: The Beginning of a New Era for the Catholic Missions in China, 1926" in Cindy Yik-Yi CHU (ed.) Catholicism in China, 1900 – Present (New York: Palgrave Macmillan, 2014), pp. 87-104.

the vicar general Domingos de Sousa, and erected for them the first church in Cochin. He sent Fr. John de Rosario to Persia and Ormuz, which developed into a center for the Persian and Arabian missions.

Francisco de Almeida (1450-1510) in 1505 also had Franciscans on board, as had Tristão da Cunha (1406-1540), who converted the mosque of Socotra into a church in honor of the Blessed Virgin in 1506.

When Alburquerque occupied Malacca in 1511 (present Melaka on the western coast of Malaysia), there were some eight priests with him, among whom six Franciscans (Fr. João Alemão), the Dominican Domingos de Souza, the secular priest Alvaro Maraglhães (Mergulhão).

The embassy of Tomé Pires (ca. 1465-1524 or 1540) as ambassador to China with Fernão Peres de Andrade as chief of the large expedition (June 1517), seems to have in his company the above Fr Alvaro Maraglhães who may have been the first known Catholic priest to enter China. However, in the first conflict between Chinese and Portuguese ships, the battle of Xicaowan in 1521, Fr. Alvaro lost his life.[38]

Malacca became soon a center for further expansion in the Far East, mainly to China and Japan: fleets were always accompanied by the clergy, secular and religious, in order to administer the Sacraments to the Portuguese and to spread the Christian faith, wherever their ships found a place to trade and to settle down: Tamão, Xiamen Bay, Ningbo (with a rather consistent Catholic community, with two churches cared by Fr. Estevão Nogueira, Shangchuan (where St. Francis died in 1552). Lampacao, Macau, where the Portuguese Fr. Gregorio Gonzales from Malacca was the first diocesan priest to settle and to work.

In 1533 Goa was separated from the Funchal Diocese, on Madeira Island (established in 1514), and the Franciscan John Alburquerque was placed in charge of the enormous new diocese, which extended from the Cape of Good Hope to Japan.

Malacca was made diocese, suffragan of Goa, in 1557, comprising the whole Far East. In 1567, Bishop Melchior Carneiro (1516-1583) was delegated by the Pope to exercise ministry in China and Japan, from Macau. On January 23, 1576, the Diocese of Macau was formally established cov-

---

[38] Manuel Texeira, *The Fourth Centenary of the Jesuits at Macao*, Macau: Salesian School, 1964, p. 7.

50

ering the whole of the Far East (Indochina, China, Mongolia, Korea and Japan), as suffragan of Goa.

About the Spanish missionary efforts, Spain's expansion started in 1519 and within two years Hernan Cortès (1485-1547) conquered the Aztec state in Mexico, called Nueva España (the New Spain). His expedition included a friar, Bartolomé de Olmedo and a priest, Juan Diaz. Conversion of the Indians was part of their mandate. Between 1519 and 1524 when 12 Franciscan friars arrived in Nueva España, which gradually became the gateway to both South America (starting with Perù), and to the Far East, with the conquest of the Philippine Islands.

In the Americas,

"Up to 1544 the dioceses in New Spain were:- Puebla, erected in 1526 at Tlaxcala, translated to Puebla, 1539 (with Fray Julian Garces as bishop*), - Mexico, 1530 (with* Fray Juan de Zumárraga, as its first Bishop*); Guatemala, 1534; - Oaxaca, erected with the title of Antequera in 1535; - Michoacan, erected in 1536 at Tzintzuntzan, translated later to Patzcuaro, and from there to the new city of Valladolid, now Morelia (with* D. Vasco de Quiroga, as the first bishop of Michoacan*); - Chiapas, 1546. They were all suffragan of the Archdiocese of Seville in Spain. Yucatán, though erected first, never had any resident bishop until 1561. On 31 January, 1545, at the solicitation of Charles V, the Holy Father, Paul III, separated these dioceses from the metropolitan See of Seville and erected the Archdiocese of Mexico, with the above-mentioned dioceses as suffragan. Before the end of the sixteenth century the ecclesiastical Province of Mexico included, besides those already mentioned, the Diocese of Comayagua in Honduras, erected 1539; Guadalajara, 1548; Verapaz in Guatemala, erected in 1556, suppressed 1605... "* [39]

As far as the Philippines are concerned, the expedition of Fernand Magellan (1480-1521) to the Philippines Islands in 1519-1522, followed by that of Juan Garcia Jofre de Loaysa (in 1525), and that of Alvaro Saavedra (in 1527) had clergy with them. A further expedition left Mexico on November 1, 1542, led by Ruy Lopez de Villalobos, which touched the Philippines and reached the Moluccas in 1544, with four Augustinian fathers, Jeronimo Jimenez, Nicolas de Perea, Sebastian de Trasierra and Alonso de Alcarado (Alvarado).

---

[39] See website "Mexico" of the New Advent Catholic Encyclopedia.

A further expedition led by Miguel Lopez de Legazpi (1502-1572) left Mexico on 21 November 1564: with him, there were other Augustinian friars, under the leadership of Andres de Urdaneta, namely Frs. Martin de Rada (Herrada), Andres de Aguirre, Diego de Herrera and Pedro de Gamboa, who built a church and convent in Cebu dedicated to the Holy Child, thus promoting the evangelization of the country.

Manila was established as a diocese, suffragan to Mexico, on February 6, 1579, by Pope Gregory XIII, with Fray Domingo Salazar, OP (1512-1594) as its bishop: he took possession of his ecclesiastical seat at his arrival on 17 September 1581, with his confrere-secretary, Fr. Christoval de Salvatierra, and the first 4 Jesuits, Frs. Antonio Sedeno and Alonso Sanchez, a brother and a scholastic.

Evangelization Methods

The most common evangelization methods under the civil patronage system were destroying the local religions with their structures and customs (the so-called *tabula rasa* way) and administering baptism in mass. These ways were used especially in America.[40]

The tabula rasa method depended on the forced relationships between the conquerors and the natives, as well as on the assumption that local cultures and traditions were of demoniac origin and, therefore, intrinsically evil. About mass baptisms, some reports speak about 14,000 baptisms in a day, or one million in a year. Though these figures should be taken with caution, the fast rhythm of baptisms without a proper preparation, allowed the ancient religious beliefs and practices to survive under a veneer of Christianity.

In the East the method of mass baptisms was limited, mainly due to the fact that Portuguese did not conquer the whole country and met with more institutionalized societies. However, they also did not pay great attention to a good preparation of the catechumens.

---

[40] Massimo MARCOCCHI, "The Missionary Elan in the Church in the 16th and 17th Centuries", in T. LIPIELLO – R. MALEK, Scholar from the West: Giulio Aleni S.J. (1582-1649) and the Dialogue between Christianity and China (Fondazione Bresciana, Brescia – Monumenta Serica Institute, Sankt Augustin, 1997), pp. 59-62.

"The priests whom the Portuguese brought with them as chaplains do not seem to be worried to deepen the beliefs of the pagans. This clergy were not lacking of zeal for baptizing the pagans, but they did it in a rather hastier pace than necessary. They were aware that the King of Portugal was quite concerned that the work of conversion should have been pushed on actively, and the good Christians were not lacking who took up seriously these royal requests. In Goa, Malacca, Moluccas, in the Chinese settlements, they planted crosses, administered baptisms to people who could understand just few words of the language; then, they departed and never reappeared again. Once baptized, the local people did not become only children of God; they, more or less, were transformed into subjects of Portugal, or, at least, they were introduced into the sphere of influence of the 'Very Faithful King'. Usually, the newly baptized received a Portuguese name: Manoel Fernandez, Duarte Barbosa, Francisco Alvarez, etc.; at times, they were forced to adopt the dress of their masters. A witness with a sensitive critical sense, the Dominican Gaspar da Cruz, has remarked that, in the Portuguese India and at Goa, the majority of the Christians was constituted by the residents of the forts and of the villages conquered: elsewhere, in Bengal, Java, Pegu. In China... they are recruited everywhere by means of slavery..."[41]

The common attitude toward local culture, even for Chinese culture, which was admittedly recognized as very rich and superior, compared with the other lands just discovered, was clearly expressed by the Memorial of 1586 *Audencia* in Manila:

"... It will be necessary to establish immediately a large number of schools, where our writing, language, and literature may be easily and quickly learned, having them abandon their own, which are extremely difficult, so much so that even they cannot understand them, while still children. These are a diabolic invention to keep them busy all their lives with their whole minds, so that they can neither go on to other sciences, nor can others teach them, without first ridding them of this hindrance. Once rid of it, not only the children, but even the grown persons of all ages will learn our letters, language, and literature — as well on account of the ease of our writing, and the relief from the burden of the other, as because of their natural aptitude, the gentleness of their dispositions, and their natural adaptability to guidance, when there is a hand to guide."[42]

---

[41] H. BERNARD, *Aux Portes de la Chine, Les Missionaires du XVI siècle, 1514-1588* (Tientsin, Haute Etudes, 1933), p. 9.

[42] See full text in http://www.fullbooks.com/The-Philippine-Islands-1493-18983.html (part 3).

In conclusion, the evangelization methods were centered upon a negative attitude toward the local religion and the administration of baptism, but without great care for the proper instruction of the neophytes. Due to the shortage of missionaries, the contacts with them were necessarily reduced, in the best cases, to once or twice per year and, therefore, their assimilation of the Christian faith was rather slow, superficial and based upon devotional practices, strongly mixed up with local religious elements.

3

ST. FRANCIS XAVIER (1506-1552) AND HIS CHINA ADVENTURE

The desire and the decision to go to China

On 29th January, 1552, from Cochin, India, Francis Xavier,[43] having already taken the decision to go to China, wrote to Europe providing some information about China and its people, as well as his plan to get there:[44]

"Opposite to Japan lies China, an immense empire, enjoying profound peace, and which, as the Portuguese merchants tell us, is superior to all Christian states in the practice of justice and equity. The Chinese whom I have seen in Japan and elsewhere, and whom I got to know, are white in color, like the Japanese, are smart, and eager to learn. Their intellect is superior even to the Japanese. Their country abounds in plenty of all things, and very many cities of great extent cover its surface. The cities are very populous; the houses ornamented with stone roofs, and very elegant. All reports say that the empire is rich in every sort of produce, but especially in silk.
I find, from the Chinese themselves, that amongst them may be found many people of many different nations and religions, and, as far as I could gather from what they said, I suspect that among them are Jews and Mahometans. Nothing leads me to suppose that there are Christians there.

---

[43] Francis Xavier (1506-1552): Spanish Jesuit missionary, one of the first members of the Society of Jesus. He was born in the Castle of Xavier near Sanguesa, in Navarre, on April 7, 1506. After his studies in Paris, where he joined Ignatius of Loyola and other to found the Society of Jesus, he left Lisboa in 1541, and stopped in Mozambique until March 1542. Then he arrived in Goa on May 6, 1542. In spring 1545 he went to Malacca and, from there, in January 1546, to the Moluccas islands. In June 1547 he returned to Malacca and, then, to India to get ready for the journey to Japan, He arrived there on August 15, in 1549. From Japan he went back to India toward the end of 1551 to prepare the journey to China. He left Goa in April 1552 and reached Shangchuan island in October 1552, but he died there on December 3, 1552, without achieving his plan to enter into the Chinese Empire.

[44] This letter, as well as all the following ones, are found in H.T. Coleridge, *The Life and Letters of St. Francis Xavier*, in www.archive.org/details/thelifeandlettersofst02coleuof.

*I hope to go there during this year [1552], and reach even to the Emperor himself.
China is that sort of kingdom, that, if the seed of the Gospel is once sown, it may
be propagated far and wide. And moreover, if the Chinese accept the Christian
faith, the Japanese would give up the doctrines which the Chinese have taught them.
Japan is separated from Liampou [Ningbo], which is a principal town in China,
by a distance of about 300 miles of sea. I am beginning to have great hopes that
God will soon provide free entrance to China, not only to our Society, but to religious
of all Orders, that a large field may be laid open to pious and holy men of all sorts,
in which there may be great room for devotion and zeal, in recalling men who are
now lost to the way of truth and salvation. I again and again beg all who have a
zeal for the spreading of the Christian faith to help by their holy sacrifices and
prayers these poor efforts of mine, that I may throw open an ample field to their
pious labors.”*

Why and when has Francis reached the decision to go to China?

It has been a rather slow process. It started out of curiosity, raised by
people talking about China, its Empire and its people, and by meeting personally some Chinese, since he reached Malacca (present Melaka, Malaysia)
in October 1545, where quite a good number of Chinese merchants were
trading. He was then informed about the 'probable' presence of Christians
in China. This increased his concern.

It was in a letter to the Society in Rome, dated May 10, 1546, from Am-
boyna (present Ambon) in the islands of the Moluccas, that Francis informed that he heard from a merchant who has been in China that up on
a mountain there is a group of people who are not Muslims but do not eat
pork and have special celebrations:

*“When the merchant told me this, I could not make a satisfactory conjecture
whether these might be some of the Christians who unite the rites of the Hebrew
law with the religion of Christ, as we know that the Ethiopians who live on the
shore of the Red Sea do, or whether they were Jews, some of whom are scattered over
all the world. I hear that all are agreed that they are not Muslims.”*

From Kagoshima, in November 1549, after he had been two and three
months in Japan, having arrived at that port on August 15, Francis wrote
to the Society members in Goa the account of his seven-week voyage between Malacca and Japan, in which he sailed along the coasts of China,
passing Canton and Tchin-tcheou (probably Quanzhou, Bay of Xiamen in
Fujian) but without stopping.

After the arrival in Japan in 1549, where he worked for more than two years, the relationship between Japan and China and the dependence of the Japanese culture upon Chinese culture increased Francis' interest for China, although in a rather superficial and subjective way, playing down the difficulties.

In fact, from Kagoshima, in November 1549, Francis wrote about the possibility to have missionaries working in Japan and in China, since

"it is said that it is easy to enter China from Japan without any fear of hurt from the natives, if you have the public guarantee of the King of Japan, whom we hope, if so, it please God, to find well disposed towards us, and whose friendship also we hope to use for that purpose. For the King of Japan is a friend of the King of China, and on account of the friendship between them he is said to have with him a ring and seal, in order that he may give to his subjects who are going to China a public passport signed by the royal seal. It is said that a good many Japanese ships sail to China, with a voyage of ten or twelve days."

The motivations of his decision

According to Fr. Matteo Ricci, the reason of the decision of St. Francis to go to China was to hasten the conversion of Japan:

"The first who gave start to this war [against Chinese paganism] *and began to pull down the wall was our Blessed Francis Xavier. He, having founded the Christian communities in India and in the Moluccas, lastly went to found that of Japan, with the optimism that his apostolic spirit hoped. And while he carried on this commitment in those kingdoms, a doubt was raised in him by their sages: 'If the faith he was preaching was so good and in accordance to reason, for which motivations the Kingdom of China, which is considered the wisest of all the oriental countries, has not yet accepted it?' And, being the Blessed Father* [Francis Xavier] *in full acquaintance that all the laws and rites of Japanese had origin from China, he realized that, if he could first convert China, not only he would achieve the greatest and noblest advantage for that kingdom, but, at the same time, Japan also should be easily converted. For this reason, entrusting all the work and affairs to other companions, who were operating there, he went back to India, where with great fastness he obtained from the Viceroy to arrange an embassy to the King of China on behalf*

of the King of Portugal, in whose occasion he could enter that kingdom and start the spreading of the Holy Gospel." [45]

The psychological reason, which convinced Francis to go to China, according to James Brodrick, was the following:

"Francis found it difficult to conceive that a civilized country, such as Japan, plainly was without a central authority and he underwent a great deal of suffering and hardship in his attempts to find the non-existent potentate. When at last he became cognizant of the real state of affairs, we observe him turning his thoughts towards China, the millennial tutor of Japan, where there reigned the emperor of his dreams. The idea at the back of his mind was perfectly sound and remained the guiding principle of later great men such as Matteo Ricci. Life was brief and eternity long. The kingdom of God must be established in the whole world, and the only swift and effective means to achieve that glorious and passionately desired end was to win to Christ the man at the top, the 'King' of Japan or the Emperor of China, or, if that proved impossible, at least to render them friendly to the Christian message." [46]

However, the most probable motivation of the decision of St. Francis seems to be his apostolic zeal: he was in charge of the evangelization of all the newly discovered countries and felt the responsibility of, at least, visiting them, in order to gain some acquaintance with the whole area entrusted to him. Joseph Sebes provides more details:

"The voyage undertaken by Xavier must not be considered as the manifestation of the spirit of adventure in this man from Navarre. Neither can it be explained solely by his desire, as Superior of the vast territories stretching from the Cape of Good Hope to Japan, to visit all his subjects and to inspect their work. He never regarded himself as an individual missionary. His task was that of a pioneer, a path-finder, destined to open the way for others. That was the work entrusted to him by the Holy See and by his own Superior, Ignatius of Loyola. Xavier was then forty-five years of age, and there seemed to him ample time to plot the course of this mighty undertaking. He was urged on by his search for a vantage point from which the

---

[45] Pasquale D'Elia, *Fonti Ricciane, 3 vols.* (Rome: La Libreria dello Stato, 1942-49), vol. I. no. 201, pp. 136-138.

[46] James Brodrick, *Saint Francis Xavier* (New York: Image Books, 1957), p. 219.

Christianization of the East could be accomplished… The Japanese themselves told him that their teachers and masters were the Chinese. Thus, after immense labors, he arrived at the conclusion that the conversion of the East Asia had to be accomplished by first converting China." [47]

The practical way: the embassy

As regards the practical way to carry out his plan, Francis, in Japan, at first, had no clear ideas, probably just thinking about some kind of an official initiative by the Portuguese Viceroy of the Indies. Leaving Japan for India, Francis reached Shangchuan island on December 17, 1551. Here the plan assumed more realistic features. Francis found in Shangchuan an old and faithful friend from Cochin, Diogo Pereira, waiting for a favorable wind to take his ship, the Santa Cruz, back to Malacca. The Portuguese at Shangchuan were considered a kind of smugglers, if not pirates, in the Chinese eyes, since normal trade with the merchants of China had been forbidden by the emperor under pain of death or life imprisonment. Several of the foreigners had been caught and languished in the jails of Canton. By some means or other, one of those unfortunate prisoners managed to smuggle out a letter to Diogo Pereira, begging him to get himself officially appointed Portuguese ambassador to the court of Peking, for only by such a move could the prisoners be saved from their terrible fate and the legal trade with China opened. Pereira showed the letter to Francis: it caused a turning point in his mind and made him think about an embassy.

Francis, though full of enthusiasm for an official embassy, sensed however that he should meet with some opposition. He raised his perplexities, when he discussed the project with Diego Pereira on his voyage from Shangchuan to Malacca, as well as during their stay in this city, which they reached on December 27. However, from Malacca, early in 1552, Francis had to depart from Diego Pereira. Diego took his ship to Sunda Kelapa (present Jakarta), while Francis left for India. They planned to meet again in Malacca, after Francis should have returned from India with the official

---

[47] Joseph Sebes, "The Precursors of Ricci", in The Jesuits 1593-1994, *Macao and China, East meets West* (*Review of Culture*, No. 21 (2nd Series) English Edition, 1994, pp. 59-60.

patent and letters constituting his friend the Envoy to China, as well as with the rich presents and other necessities for the expedition.

In Goa, the project of the embassy to China encountered no obstacle. The Viceroy gave the patents, which constituted Diogo Pereira ambassador of Portugal to the Chinese Court, and he added strong letters to the Commandant of Malacca, ordering him to favor the expedition in every possible manner. Pereira had given Francis letters of credit on his agent in Goa for thirty thousand ducats, in order to purchase rich presents for the Chinese Emperor, as well as for the other necessary expenses. The royal treasury also contributed to the cost, and a good sum was raised among pious and charitable persons for the general purposes of the voyage, which included also the liberation of a number of Portuguese prisoners. Everything seemed to promise well, although several people expressed their apprehension.

On February 1, from Cochin, Francis wrote to Fr. Simon Rodriguez in Portugal:

"Many friends and those who are devoted to me are appalled by my undertaking such a long and dangerous voyage. But I am more terrified than them at seeing what little faith they have, since God our Lord has power and dominion over the tempests of the seas of China and Japan, which are the greatest that have yet been seen…"

Early April 1552, Francis clarified the recent events and his plan for China, in a letter to St. Ignatius:

"After six days, if God approves, we shall go three of the Society, two of whom are priests. to the kingdom of China. This kingdom, which is very large, lies opposite Japan. It is crowded to a very great degree with men of sharp wits and much learning. As far as I have been able to find out, studies flourish there, and in proportion as a man is more learned, in that same degree does he surpass the rest in rank and influence. It is well enough ascertained that the religions which exist in Japan have been brought from China. We go full of hope and confidence in God, and we trust that the name of Christ will at last make its way into China."

On April 10, from Goa, Francis updated also the King John of Portugal on the details and the nature, both political and religious, of the embassy:

"In five days, I shall leave Goa for Malacca, on the way to China, with a brother of our Society, and also with Diego Pereira, ambassador to the emperor of that

country. We are taking to these Sovereign rich presents, bought by Diogo Pereira, partly with your Highness's funds, partly with his own. But we carry him another present, such as perhaps within the memory of man, no king has ever offered to another king, I speak of the Gospel of Jesus Christ. If the Emperor of China understands its full value, he will certainly prefer it above all his treasures, however great they may be... Three of us all of the Society start with Pereira for China, in order to set at liberty, the Portuguese who are in captivity there, to obtain the alliance of the Emperor of China for the Portuguese, and lastly to wage war with the devil and his followers..."

Francis Xavier took his final leave of India on April 25. He had with him Father Balthasar Gago and three scholastics, Duarte de Silva, Pedro de Alcageva, and Alvaro Ferreira, as well as a young Chinese named Antonio, as interpreter, who had been educated in the College of Santa Fe'.

The journey to China

Francis Xavier embarked with an optimistic heart. He was in the vigor of life, still in the prime of his years, his heart full of great plans, with his prestige quite established all over the Far East. He has always been able to obtain what he asked from the Portuguese authorities; and the charm of his holiness and charity made everybody, merchants, sailors, and soldiers eager to befriend him.

The voyage was peaceful, except near the Nicobar Islands, when they met with a storm. On arriving at Malacca, they found the plague raging. Forty of the crew of the ship soon died. Francis devoted himself at once to the service of the sick people. As the hospital was full to overflowing, he gave up a part of the residence of the Society, where more than fifty were received at a time. He was always ready to hear the confessions of the sick, and to assist the dying.

Diogo Pereira returned to Malacca from Sunda, after Francis had been some time in the city. Then, troubles started. At that time, in Malacca, Don Alvaro d'Ataide de Gama, son of the famous Vasco de Gama, was taking up full power. He was proud and ambitious, since he had succeeded to oust Pedro de Silva before his period of Captaincy had elapsed. He was probably also poor and anxious to make money while in authority at Malacca. He had a secret grudge against Diogo Pereira, who, before sailing for Sunda, had refused to lend him a sum of ten thousand ducats. Moreover, he was envious of him and thought that the role of ambassador should be taken up by himself. The Captaincy of the sea gave Alvaro authority over the vessels in the port, and he availed himself of it. The first exercise of his authority was to seize the rudder of Pereira's vessel. He did not allow Pereira to take Francis to China, under many pretexts.

It was then that, for the first time since he had left Portugal, Francis Xavier made public the appointment as Apostolic Nuncio, received by the Pope Paul III at the request of the King. When he landed in India, he had informed the bishop of the briefs which he possessed, but from that time he had kept silence on the subject. He now communicated the briefs to the Vicar of Malacca, Joan Suarez, and begged him to inform Don Alvaro of the danger he was in: by impeding an Apostolic Nuncio to carry out his mission he was solemnly excommunicated by the Pope. He would not allow it to be passed over in silence that he was already excommunicated by the Church and the Roman Pontiff, if he persisted in his opposition to his voyage to China. The excommunication was formally intimated to Don Alvaro.

Don Alvaro treated the Pontifical briefs with the same disrespect as the order of the Viceroy; he went so far as to even accuse Francis of having forged the documents. But, at last, he consented as a compromise to allow Francis to go to Shangchuan on the ship of 'Santa Crux' but without Pereira. There would be no embassy, but the missionary would be allowed to proceed on his path. Alvaro even seized the ship and the merchandize, leaving only a small part to Pereira, and he put on board, along with a portion of Pereira as crew, some people of his own, instructing them to show little respect to Francis. Pereira seems to have behaved nobly. Francis, before leaving, sent a moving thanksgiving message to him for his kindness.[48]

From Malacca to Shangchuan Island

Francis left Malacca in July. The 'Santa Crux' soon reached Singapore, and stopped there several days, during which Francis wrote some letters to express his disappointment. On July 20, 1552, he wrote to Caspar Baertz,

---

[48] See Letter cix. "From our house at Malacca, on the point of embarking in your ship. June 25, 1552. Francis to Diego Pereira."

Rector of the College at Goa informing him of the disappointing obstacles he met and that he has kept with him only Fr. Alvaro Ferreira and Antonio the Chinese interpreter, sending all the other three fathers to Japan.

On August 1, 1552, always from Singapore, Francis wrote to Diogo Pereira:

"I have been thinking that it would be well, Senor, if you wrote yourself to the King at full length, and minutely dwelling on all the advantages which could not fail to accrue to the Portuguese interests from the establishment of commerce with China, and if a residence were obtained for the King's officers in the port of Canton. I should like you to write on the same subject, and as carefully, to the Viceroy of India. For I am writing myself to the King in the same tone, as you may see by the letters, which I send open. You will read and seal them..."

On Shangchuan Island

Francis reached Shangchuan island in the last week of August 1552. Not long after, he fell ill with a fever, which kept him to his bed for a fortnight. Then, he tried with the help of some Portuguese to find a way to Canton. Towards the end of October, he wrote the letters, which show his expectations for entering China.

On October 21, 1552, Francis wrote to Diogo Pereira, explaining his situation and plans. On the following day, October 22, 1552, he gave more details of the events after his arrival at Shangchuan, to his confrere Fr. Francis Perez, who was in charge of the work in Malacca:

"By the grace of God all of us have reached safely the port of San Chuan, 120 miles from Canton. On disembarking I had a hut made as a chapel, in which I offered the Holy Sacrifice every day till I fell ill. I suffered altogether for a fortnight from fever, and now by God's goodness I am restored to health. I do not want for holy occupations. I hear confessions, appease quarrels, and do other things of that sort. A great number of Chinese merchants from Canton come to this island for the sake of commerce, and the Portuguese have often dealt with them diligently to procure my passage to Canton; but they have all flatly refused, declaring that it would be at great risk to their lives and property if the governor of that town should hear of it, and it was impossible to persuade them to receive us on board of their junks. However, doubtless by God's arrangement, we have met with an honest Canton merchant, who has come to an agreement with me for 200 gold pieces (cruzados).

He promises to take us in a little vessel, which is to carry no one else but his own sons and a few faithful slaves; so that if the governor of the town ever gets to hear of the affair, he will not be able to find out from the crew who took us to Canton. He has also promised that we shall be in his house for three or four days, with our books and baggage; and then very early one morning he is to take us to the gate of the town and put us on the road leading to the government house. I shall go straight to the governor, telling him that I have come to announce the divine and heavenly law to the Emperor of China, and then I shall produce the Bishop of Goa's letters addressed to that monarch. All the Chinese merchants are always glad to see us, and say they shall be very glad if the matter is accomplished.

I am aware, as all tell me, of the twofold danger of this enterprise. It is possible that the Chinese merchant after receiving the gold may leave us in a desert island, or throw us into the sea to conceal his crime; and again, if we reach Canton, the governor may put us to all kinds of unheard-of tortures, or make slaves of us for life. It is a capital crime for a foreigner to enter any part of China without a passport. However, there are other dangers besides, greater and more unknown, all of which I cannot enumerate to you, but I will mention a few of them..."

On November 12, 1552, Francis again updated Fr. Francis Perez in Malacca:

"I have been expecting for a week the merchant who is to take me secretly to the city of Canton. I have the fullest confidence in his return, unless some hindrance should occur beyond the power of man to overcome, and I rely on the great value of the reward which I have promised him, and which he highly appreciates himself; for the quantity of pepper which I have agreed to have delivered to him, if he conveys me safe and sound to Canton, will easily obtain for him a profit of more than 350 gold pieces of our money. I have to thank my very dear friend Diogo Pereira for the means of buying my passage to China at so high a price, and he has of his own accord, and with great generosity, placed at my disposal this large quantity of very valuable merchandize. May God reward him, as I cannot, for I shall owe him a debt, I can never repay all my life...

There are three of us, Antonio of the Santa Fe' College, Cristoval, and myself... Should it happen that the Chinese merchant, on whom depend our hopes of going to Canton, should change his mind through fear or any other reason, and break his word, I have resolved in this last case to sail for the kingdom of Siam, for which voyage I have a favorable opportunity. In fact, I have heard that a ship was being fitted out there for Canton, and if I can get on board, by God's protection I hope before the end of the year to land on the shore which is the object of so many prayers to me..."

On November 12, 1552, Francis wrote to Diogo Pereira, about an alternative plan for the embassy for the following year.

November 13 is the date of the last two letters of St. Francis, one to Father Caspar Baertz and the second to the same and to Fr. Francesco Perez.

"I have written to Francesco Perez, telling him to leave Malacca at once, and go to India with all his brothers. I think that at this time that city is unworthy of so great a blessing, after having been the occasion of so great a misfortune, hindering by exceeding wickedness our voyage to China and the extension of God's glory. I again enjoin you to carry out my last order with great zeal and diligence; that is to say, to arrange with the Lord Bishop that he may have the excommunications incurred by those who prevented our voyage to China solemnly pronounced in Malacca; for I was on my way to China in the character of Apostolic Nuncio. I insist on this point on two grounds: first, because I want the Governor of Malacca to be made to understand the gravity both of the crime he has committed and of the penalty he has incurred, so that he may not in future act to anyone else as he has acted to me; secondly, that no one may venture to stop those members of our Society who may later on go to Malacca, to the Moluccas, to Japan, or to China, in the interests of religion. And as nowadays most men are more restrained by disgrace before the world than before God, I desire all such persons to be frightened by such a mark of infamy and ignominy from acting with such outrageous audacity…"

In the last letter, Francis continued his instructions to the two fathers:

"… With regard to myself, I have written this letter in the midst of preparations and anxieties relating to my passage from this island to the Chinese continent. The voyage will be most painful under my present strained circumstances; it is full of a thousand dangers, of very doubtful issue, and full of terrors. How it will turn out I know not, but I have a firm confidence, and a strong inward assurance, that however things may go, the result will be good. If, which God forbid, my hopes of the Canton merchant captain, whom I expect every moment, should fail, I am determined, as I told you, to go by sea to Siam, whence there is some expectation of being able to get to China. Should this hope to come to nothing, through some accident, then I shall return to India. But my mind presages that I shall not be driven to this last resolution, and I persist in believing that my first hope will be fulfilled, and that I shall have my prayer and place my foot at last on Chinese ground…"

Death and Burial

A few days after the writing of these letters, Francis was again struck by fever. It was on November 21, after he has said Mass for a man who recently has died on the island. There was scarcity of provisions on the island, and Francis suffered privation. The day in which the Chinese merchant had promised to appear passed on. The interpreter on whom Francis had reckoned had already given up the design for lack of courage. Only hope remained. When the fever first attacked him, Francis asked to be brought on board of the Santa Crux: but the motion of the ship made the situation more difficult, and he begged to be taken ashore. He arrived there in so high a fever that a Portuguese merchant compassionately took him into his own hut. He went on suffering through the week; lying in the wood cabin, gazing up to heaven through a small window and talking with the devotion to a little Crucifix he kept in his hand. On the Monday week after his illness had begun, he became delirious for a time. He lost his speech, but on Thursday he regained it. He begged that the vestments and the sacred vessels which he has used for Mass, as well as his manuscript of the Christian doctrine in Chinese should be taken on board of the ship. Antonio, the Chinese lad and Cristoval, the Malabar man, were his only attendants. He prayed a good deal in ejaculations, chiefly in Latin, until the night of Friday. Toward the dawn of Saturday, December 3, with his eyes fixed upon his Crucifix, his face lighting up, he breathed his last, repeating the words of the Te Deum, *In te Domine speravi, non confundar in aeternum.*

The body of Francis Xavier remained unburied until Sunday. Some of the Portuguese of the ship were touched at the sight of his corpse. Antonio, the pilot Francesco d'Aghiar and Jorge Alvarez had a coffin made, in which the body was placed, clothed in the priestly vestments; they thought well to cover it with lime, in order that the flesh might be soon consumed and the bones taken to India. Late on Sunday evening, the coffin was lowered into a grave dug on a level space on the slope of the hill. Only four people followed Francis to the grave.

When the ship had to depart on February 17, 1553, Antonio asked the captain to examine the state of the bones of Francis. But when the coffin was opened, and the lime removed, the body was found entirely fresh. The body was put as it was in a coffin on board of 'Santa Crux', which sailed immediately and, after a good voyage, reached Malacca on March 22, 1553.

The body of Francis was taken out of the coffin, and buried in the doorway to the sacristy of the church. It remained until August 1553, when Diogo Pereira put him in a magnificent coffin and kept him in his house until the departure for India on December 11. In January 1554, the vessel arrived at Cochin, from where a galley sent from Goa, reached this harbor on Holy Thursday, March 15, 1554, where he received a solemn welcome and burial.

The desire and decision to reach and enter China of St. Francis Xavier did not die with him: it passed on to his confreres of the Society of Jesus. Fr. Ricci later wrote:

> " *... all the Blessed Father's stratagems for entering China fell to the ground. Yet, we believe that, if he could not obtain from God the privilege for himself, he obtained it in heaven for his companions, who, against all human hope, succeeded thirty years later.* " [49]

---

[49] P. D'Elia, *Fonte Ricciane*, o.c., I, no. 201, p. 139.

4

MISSIONARY ATTEMPTS IN CHINA (XVI CENTURY)

Papal wavering legislation

Following the political expansion, both Portuguese and Spanish missionaries made several attempts to reach and enter the Chinese Empire, in view of beginning its evangelization.

The vicar-general of the Order of the Augustinians, Pedro de Herrera, since February 5, 1564, has received from Pope Pius IV (1499-1565, r. since 1559) the confirmation of all the privileges and authorities given by the previous Popes, for "all brethren going to the countries of unbelievers, to preach the Holy Gospel of Christ – especially to Farther Tartaria, China and other regions of the earth…" [50]

Pope Gregory XIII (1502-1585, r. since 1572), in September and October 1582, issued two documents[51] allowing the foundation of the Dominican mission with the appointment of its vicar-general, "in the Philippine Island and in the kingdom of China".

There was no restriction for any missionary to go to China, except those imposed by the Portuguese and Spanish governments, as well as by the Chinese authorities themselves. However, the Jesuits obtained from Gregory XIII with the Brief *Ex Pastorali Officio* (28 January 1585) the exclusive right for the evangelization of Eastern Asia, namely China and Japan, forbidding to all clergy "of whatsoever order, standing, degree rank and condition – under pain of major excommunication to be incurred ipso facto to this effect: that without his express license and that of the Apostolic See, no one should dare go to the aforesaid countries and provinces to preach the Gospel…".

---

[50] Letter to the confreres, reported in Emma Helen Blair & James Alexander Robertson (eds), *The Philippine Islands, 1493-1898,* 55 vols., http://philhist.pbworks.com/w/page/16367055/ThePhilippineIslands, vol. 2, p. 167.

[51] Blair & Robertson, o.c., vol 5, pp. 200-291.

On April 12, 1586, the Viceroy of India Don Duarte de Meneses, prohibited the entry in China and Japan of all missionaries except the Jesuits.

This situation, however, was short-lived. Sixtus V (1521-1590, r. since 1585) with the Bull *Dum ad uberes* (15 November 1586) raised the custody of St. Gregory the Great in the Philippines of the Franciscans to the grade of province, separating it from the province of St. Joseph in Spain, and giving them the right to open convents and churches 'in every part' of the Orient.

"In words truly weighty and worthy of so great a pontiff, he charged this province and its superiors with the zeal that they ought to have in attending to the conversions in their care. His Holiness especially charged the conversion of the great empire of China upon them." [52]

The Franciscans, in fact, interpreted this Bull as a derogation, at least for them, of the Brief of Gregory XIII, and the same was understood in Manila.

Later, Pope Clement VIII (1536-1605, r. since 1592), by the Constitution *Onerosa Pastoralis Officii* (12 December 1600), granted to all superiors general of religious congregations the right to send their members in these countries, provided that they will start the journey from Lisboa and Goa. All other ways were interdicted: he forbade those who under *"no matter what pretext or color of design, to leave the islands known as the Philippines or any other part of the Western Indies (Mexico) and thence to pass to the said Japanese Islands, provinces, and countries or other near-by lands..."*

However, this clause was abolished by Paul V (1550-1621, r. since 1605) in 1608 with the Constitution *Sedis Apostolicae*, given under the request of the Franciscans and of the Court of Madrid. So, it became possible for the missionaries to choose the route to the Far East, and this was open to the members of all religious Orders. Paul V allowed all superiors to send their members to those countries "otherwise than by way of Portugal, in all remaining matters, however being bound in all respects to observe the said letters of his predecessors..."

---

[52] "Early Franciscan Missions", reported in Blair & Robertson, o.c., vol. 35, p. 304.

On February 22, 1632, Pope Urban VIII (1568-1644, r. since 1623) gave new provisions and powers to the superiors of all orders to send any member considered suitable to those lands, provided that they follow the instruction of Pope Clement VIII. He forbade any clergy of any order and rank, under excommunication *latae sententiae*, from hindering the journey of the missionaries to those countries; in those lands, uniformity in teaching, especially in morals (following the Roman Catechism or the Christian Doctrine of Bellarmine) should be observed; he interdicted and forbade to the clergy any engagement in worldly affairs and trafficking (excommunication *latae sententiae*, *ipso facto*, also for the negligent superiors).[53]

Different instructions and confusion were caused by the lack of objective geographical knowledge: at times, the Philippines and China were known also as West Indies, confusing them with Nueva España, or Mexico.

First sporadic Missionary Attempts

The first and most famous was the attempt of St. Francis Xavier, as it has been already described in detail in the previous chapter. He unfortunately died at the door of the Chinese Empire on the island of Shangchuan, during the night between 2 and 3 December, 1552, failing to achieve his objective.

The Jesuit Bro. Peter d'Alcaçova, on his return from Japan to India, reached Shangchuan on 19 October 1553 and visited the place where St. Francis was buried staying there a week. Then he went to Malacca, from where he could accompany the corpse of Francis Xavier to India.

At about the same year, as we have already mentioned, Fr. Gregorio Gonzales was sent from Malacca and succeeded to settle in Macao where he worked as Vicar for a dozen of years.

Fr. Melchior Nuñez Barreto (1519-1571)

On 20 July 1555, Fr. Melchior Nuñez Barreto, the Portuguese provincial of the Jesuits, who has left India in May 1584 on his way to Japan and has spent the winter in Malaka, visited Shangchuan island and could celebrate

---

[53] See the text in Blair & Robertson, o.c., vol. 24, pp. 263-272.

Mass on the former tomb of St. Francis Xavier. He was accompanying two other confreres, Frs. Gaspar Villela (1526-1572) and Antonio Dias, four scholastics, Melchior Dias, Ferrante Mendez, Antonio Paez and Estaváo de Goes as well as four youths, Guillerme, Rui Pereira, Regeira and Gaspar. Shangchuan island was then the meeting place of Portuguese and Chinese traders. On August 3, Fr. Barreto went to Lampacao island about four or six leagues further north-east, where he found four hundred Portuguese sailors and merchants. They had built huts on the island. The Jesuits built a chapel, where they could celebrate Mass. There was great attendance to confessions. Fr. Barreto always stayed on the ship of Egidio de Goes and every morning landed to celebrate Mass. Fr. Gaspar Villela remained on the galleon of Francisco Toscano, with Bro. de Goes, the sacristan and the boys who were studying the Christian doctrine; Fr. Antonio Dias stayed on the galleon of Antonio Pereira, while Ferrante Mendez and Antonio Paez resided on land near the chapel, to prepare for the priests' liturgical celebrations.

Fr. Barreto decided to go to Canton with Louis de Almeida, the captain of a ship, well known to the Chinese authorities, taking also Bro. de Goes with the intention to get for him the permit to stay there and study the Chinese language. The main purpose, however, was to obtain the release from prison of three Portuguese (among whom Mattheo de Brito) and three other people. He offered for ransom amber in the first visit, and then he returned a second time with money, but to no avail.

"And invoking God's favor, he returned another time to Canton, where he stopped another month or more: and he had a commission from the Portuguese to hand a thousand and five hundred ducats for redeeming Mattheo de Brito; but the viceroy did not want, under the excuse that he needed the decision from the King, in order to understand His will about the mentioned Mattheo. In the meantime, the divine mercy gave a chance of greater hope to this man full of desire for a large number of souls, by moving a great Caziz [scholar [of high authority to hold public debate with him. More than three hundred people gathered together, among whom many Chinese literati, as judges of the debate, which soon started with great satisfaction of the assembly, in hearing the marvels of God, of His creation of the visible and invisible things, topics of which they were unaware and unfamiliar. The source of the doctrine of the Caziz dried off at the first answer, and he felt too confused, realizing that he was unable to defend himself; considering he'd better not to wait for the ending and to lose all his credit and authority, vehemently spitting almost

on the face of the father, turning his shoulders he shouted, 'the devil brought here this other devil to debate with me.' The Chinese, as soon as they saw him leaving, started in a loud voice to ridicule their Caziz and make joke of him…" [54]

On November 20, Fr. Barreto met in Macau Fernão Mendes Pinto, the writer of the 'Peregrinations': *From Lampacao, the harbor where we are staying, I have arrived here today in Amacau which is a further six leagues ahead, and where I met Master Belchior [Melchior Barreto] who reached here from Canton, where he had been for 25 days to ransom Mattheo and another man…* [55]

On November 23, Fr. Barreto informed the confreres in India about his travel and suggested possible ways to spread the Gospel in China:

"The following is the major difficulty people find in China to become Christians: that is, humanly speaking they seem lacking of enough courage to take up a new doctrine and law without the permit of those in authority: nor the latter will dare to give it without the permit of the King. Consequently, according to what I experience in this land, it seems that there are only two possible ways (both difficult) to be followed to achieve their conversion, not to speak of the grace and the intervention of the Spirit, who is always necessary in any way. The first way seems more human: it consists in negotiating an embassy to come to this Kingdom, to achieve a peaceful agreement between them and the Portuguese; together with the ambassador, some of the members of the Company should go to the place where the King resides, which is said to be a journey of a thousand and five hundred miles inland, the most of which is by the river. And since, after the arrival of the ambassador in Canton, it is required to wait for almost one year for the sending and returning of the acceptance of the request from the King, there will be time and opportunity enough to practice the language and to get acquainted with the local conditions. Then, going with the ambassador where the King lives, efforts should be done to get the license to celebrate the divine offices, to get engaged in charitable works and to edify people: and after receiving some news of their virtue through the same ambassador and even though the same members of the Company who have gone, a sealed approval

---

⁵⁴ Fr. Louis Froys (Frois 1528-1597) > to confreres of Goa St Paul's College, 7 January 1556, from Malacca, where he received all the news from a friend of the priests, who had just reached Malacca on a ship (see the Italian text of the letter in http://www.upf.edu/asia/projectes/che/che16.htm).

⁵⁵ Louis Pfister, *Notices Biographiques et Bibliographiques sur el Jesuites de l'Ancienne Mission de Chine, 1552-1773*, Tome I, Imprimerie de la Mission Catholique, Chang-hai, 1932, pp. 8-9.

could be requested from the King, that all his subjects who would like to accept the law of the Creator, could freely do it, without scandal nor prejudice for him, and that neither the Mandarins nor the other Governors could forbid it, but give favor to those who follow the Christian Religion. And so, such an undertaking could start; otherwise, neither the King nor the Mandarins would accept to dialogue, and so, there will be no chance to give account of the faith of Jesus Christ, our Savior.

The second way is not so much founded on human means and needs of fasting: it consists in this: two Fathers of the Company, knowing the two languages, should go to Canton; and when the Portuguese ships had to leave, they should remain with the risk of the canes and start to preach our most holy Faith, both in the squares and in the houses; and even if they are put into prison, they should never stop preaching the Word of God, both in favorable and adverse conditions, in consolations as well as in afflictions, proposing it with steadfast faith and hope: if the grain will die, it will produce ears and fruits. At present, it is true that I find an inconvenience for it, in the lack of language interpreters, who as young Chinese meeting with some trouble, lose their courage, have fear to declare the things of God, which are told them, and even misinterpret them; they don't have the constancy which is required to persevere...

What I feel in this land with my weak judgment is that some of the Fathers of the Company should come here, learn well the language, keep high spirit, that our Lord God might work some miracles through them and His mercy would bestow on some Chinese the grace of the faith in Jesus Christ Our Lord: in this way, many fruits will be harvested and they will increase, helping God those in authority so that they do not to put up any obstacle." [56]

Fr. Barreto went to Canton a third time in 1556 during Lent for the same above- mentioned double purpose. But, no way. Then, on June 5, he continued his journey to Japan, leaving Bro. de Goes in Macau to learn the language. Fr. Barreto reappeared back on December 4, 1556, and found the brother very ill. Therefore, he had to take him to Goa on December 24. From Cochin, on January 8, 1558, he wrote a letter in which he described the island of Lampacao, the city of Canton and the work in Japan. In another letter, dated December 31, 1561, also from Cochin, he informed about his intention to return to China in a Portuguese embassy.

Fr. Gaspar da Cruz (?- February 5, 1570)

---

[56] M. Barreto > Fathers in Goa, 23 Nov. 1555, from Macau, in Italian language (in http://www.upf.edu/asia/projectes/che/che16.htm).

During the autumn of 1556, a Portuguese Dominican, Fr. Gaspar da Cruz also reached Canton from Cambodia. He had left for India in 1548 together with the vicar general Diego Bermudes, and then, through Goa, Malacca, where he founded the Dominican convent of Our Lady of the Rosary, and Cambodia, has reached China. In Canton he started preaching, but after few weeks [57] he left, a bit discouraged. To the question why he did not remain there preaching the Gospel and converting people, he gave the following reasons:

"To this I answer that there are two very inconveniences to make any Christian in this country. The one is that in no way will they permit any novelty in the country, as in some sort it may be seen in the matter of the Moors. So that whatsoever novelty appears in the country, the Louthias [the authorities] take order forthwith how to repress it, and it goes no further… The second is, that no strange person may enter into China, nor remain in Cantam [Canton, present Guangzhou], save only with leave of the Louthias, who do give license to stay for a certain fixed time in Cantam, and when the time of the license has expired, they labor to make him depart… Add to the above said, that the common people greatly fear the Louthias, wherefore none of them dares become a Christian without their license, or at least many would not do it. Therefore, as a man cannot be settled in the country, he cannot continue preaching, and by consequence he cannot fructify and preserve the fruit. There is, notwithstanding, one way by which a man could preach freely, and whereby fruit might be made in the country, without even a dog barking at the preacher, nor any Louthia do him hurt in any way; which is, if we could have a license for it from the King. and it might be obtained of a solemn embassy were sent with a solemn present to the King of China, in the name of the King of Portugal, religious men going with the ambassador to obtain the license for going about the country, showing themselves to be men without arms; and how our faith is no prejudice to his dominion and government, but a great help that all might obey him and keep his laws. This is the only remedy that there is for to reap any fruit in China, and there is no other (humanly speaking); and without this, it is impossible for any religious

---

[57] About the length of Fr. Gaspar's stay in China, speaking about the need for a license to remain in Canton, he specified "Wherefore because I and those who were with me had been for a month in Canton, they set up written boards in the streets, that none should keep nor harbor us in their houses under pain, until we held it our best to go to the ships." Boxer, in the introduction to Gaspar's *"Tractado das Cousas da China"* (in Boxer's *South China in the Sixteenth Century*, o. c.), speaks about "few weeks in Canton", and "he was not more than a few months in China altogether".

men to preach or to fructify, and because I had not this remedy, having the above-said inconveniences, I came away from China; and therefore, neither I nor they of the Company of Jesus, who undertook this enterprise sundry times, did not achieve any fruit in China".[58]

He reached Macau, after a violent typhoon had destroyed almost all the few huts, which had been built there. He left for Malacca, probably in early 1557, since his arrival is mentioned in a letter of Luis Froys, who was then in Malacca, dated 11 November 1557. "After Father Mestre Belchior's [Melchior] departure from this land, with other brothers, who had arrived in his company from China (by whom you will know the news of this land to that time), Frei Gaspar, who from Cambodia went to China, soon arrived here".

Then, Fr. Gaspar da Crux took up residence in Ormuz and returned to Lisboa in 1569, where he published the work, "*Tractado das Cousas da China*" (Lisboa: Evora, 1569-1570), [59] the first book published in Europe totally related to China., which played a primary role in introducing China to Europe.

"[His book] may fairly be claimed as the first book devoted to China which was printed in Europe, if we except the work of Marco Polo, which, after all, dealt rather with 'the kingdoms and marvels of the East' in general than with the wonders of medieval Cathay in particular. Accounts of China had been published by the Portuguese historians Fernão Lopes de Castanheda, João de Barros and Damião de Goes, in their general histories dealing with the rise of the Portuguese power in Asia: but these accounts, like the narrative of Galeote Pereira and others which were embodied in the Jesuit annual relations, were not books on China, but only parts of books which dealt incidentally with China. Nine-tenths of Cruz's Tractado is directly concerned with China, and it is clear from his preface that he intended the book to be entirely devoted to that country… All the omissions of Marco Polo are there made good, and our friar has many observations on Chinese life and customs which anticipate those of the later Jesuits writers who are usually credited with first

---

[58] His 'Tractado', reported in C. R. Boxer, *South China in the Sixteenth Century, o.c.*, pp. 221-22. It is quoted also by Henri Bernard, *Aux Portes de la Chine, Leas Missionaires du XVI Siècle, 1514-1588* (Tientsin: Haute Etudes, 1933) p. 68.

[59] For more details about Friar Gaspar and the text of his work, see C.R. Boxer, *South China… o.c..*

revealing China to Europe. It might, perhaps, be going too far to claim that Gaspar da Cruz made better use of his few weeks' stay in Canton than did Marco Polo of all the years he spent in Cathay; but there can be no doubt that the Portuguese friar gives us a better and clearer account of China as he saw it than did the more famous Italian traveler. Writers on the history of the Far East too often assume that nothing noteworthy about China was published in Europe between the accounts of Marco Polo and those of Juan Gonzalez de Mendoza and Matteo Ricci. Woeful ignorance of Portuguese and Spanish historical literature is probably responsible for this erroneous impression, at any rate in English-speaking countries. I think that most people who have had the opportunity of traveling in China and of reading the Tractado of Gaspar da Cruz, will agree that this Portuguese account will stand comparison with any of those printed in Europe before 1625 – and with many of those printed much later." [60]

On 21 November 1560, the Jesuit father Balthasar Gago (1515-1583) with Bro. Rui Pereira, left Japan for India. On their trip they were forced by a severe storm, to seek refuge on Hainan Island until May 1561, from where, after a journey of about a month, they reached Macau and remained there until January 1, 1562.

On 24 August 1562, the Italian Jesuit, Giovanni Battista de Monte (1528-1587), together with the Portuguese confrere, Luis Froys arrived in Macau and remained there until the middle of 1563; then, they went to Japan.

On 26 July 1563, the Jesuits Francisco Perez (1514-1583), Manuel Texeira (1536-1590) and the scholastic André Pinto (1538-1588) arrived in Macau in the entourage of embassy to China of Diogo Pereira and Gil Goys. Writing from Canton, where the priests had few times accompanied the Portuguese for the trade, Fr. Texeira reported that the attempts made to proceed to Peking were unsuccessful. As we have seen, this embassy failed, but the fathers remained in Macao living in the house of Pedro Quintero and celebrating Mass there also for other people. On 15 November 1565, the Jesuits, the Spanish Juan de Escobar and the above-mentioned Francisco Perez went to Canton and on 21 November, Perez asked permission from the city authorities to remain in China, but it was refused.

---

[60] C.R. Boxer, *South China …*, o.c., Introduction, p. lxii.

Meanwhile, at the end of 1564 the Jesuits had received from their Provincial in India, Fr. Antonio de Quadros, the order to open a permanent resident for the Society. But it was only very late in 1565 that they could build the Jesuit House, at the site of the present presbytery of St. Anthony's Church, a small earth-walled house, together with their first straw church; they soon started classes for children.

Attempts of the Augustinian Fathers (1575-1576)

In the meantime, the concern for China was also growing in the Philippines among the Spanish missionaries.

"The Augustinians who accompanied Villalobos had sailed from the port of Natividad, Mexico, already with the intention of preaching the gospel in China. In 1572, Fathers Agustin de Alburquerque and Alonso de Alvarado also tried to cross into the Chinese mainland in order to announce the Good News there. The same dream inspired Father Martin de Rada together with Fr Jeronimo Marin: they succeeded in crossing the imperial frontier in 1575 as an ambassador of Philip II. But they all failed in their undertaking." [61]

In fact, in the expedition led by Miguel Lopez de Legazpi who reached Cebu on 26 April 1565, there were also Augustinian friars, under the leadership of Andres de Urdaneta, namely Frs. Martin de Rada (Herrada), Andres de Aguirre, Diego de Herrera and Pedro de Gamboa. They built a church and convent in Cebu dedicated to the Holy Child. Soon after his arrival in 1565, Fr Martin de Rada (1533-1578),[62] getting in contact with local Chinese and merchants, showed a great desire, shared by other confreres, to go to preach the Gospel to their people and started to study Chinese.

At first, the Augustinian fathers were unsuccessful in persuading the traders to embark them on their vessels. A letter written by the Governor

---

[61] Juan Gonzales de Mendoza, *Historia del gran Reyno de China* (Madrid, Pedro Madrigal Printer, 1586) reports the history of the journey. Pablo Fernandez OP, *History of the Church in the Philippines, 1521-1898* [Metro Manila: Life Today Publications, 1988], p. 287, quoting Elviro PEREZ, OSA, *Catalogo bio-bibliograifco de los religiosos agustinos* [Manila, 1901, pp. 5, 10, 26).

[62] See a biography of Fr. Rada, in Pedro G. Galende, OSA, *Apologia Pro Filipinos* (Salesiana Publishers, Manila, 1980).

Legazpi to one of the Chinese viceroys, and accompanied by a present, also failed to be delivered. It took them some time before being able to fulfill their desire. A good occasion was given by the presence of Limahon or Lin Feng, a Chinese pirate who reached the coasts of the Philippines on November 30, 1574. He set a siege to Manila, but, later, he was forced to retire to Pangasinan on the NW coast of Luzon. A Chinese war-junk arrived off the port of Manila looking for the pirate. The Chinese captain, Omocon (Wang Wanggao) was well received by the Spaniards, who promised to surrender Limahon if they caught him. At the same time, they handed over some Chinese women who had been abducted by the pirate and whom they had captured. In return, Omocon invited a Philippine delegation to meet the provincial authorities of Fujian.

So, together with Omocon on his vessels, Frs. Martin de Rada and Jeronimo Marin with two military officers, Miguel de Loarca (Lorcha), Pedro Sarmiento to whom were added Nicholas de Cuenca and John de Triana, as well as a Chinese youth as interpreter, Hernando Tang, could leave on 12 June 1575, sent by the Governor of the Philippines, Guido de Lavezares as ambassadors of Philip II. Their purpose was to get the permit for the missionaries to stay and begin the evangelization work, as well as to get a trading port for Spain. They were bringing three letters, one for the mandarins of Chincheo (Quanzhou), a second for the provincial viceroy of Fujian and third for the emperor. They reached the bay of Amoy, in the port of Tongan on July 5, (Tongcongsu, the native place of Omocon) and Quanzhou, where they were well received, and given an audience, after which they were taken to the provincial capital, Fuzhou. Here the viceroy accepted the letter and the document in which the fathers stated the purpose and the religious intention of their journey. The viceroy requested a book of the Christian doctrine and was presented with a breviary, the only book the fathers had. After hearing a brief explanation of the Christian faith, the viceroy, with the excuse of getting the permit from the emperor, he simply dismissed them, loading them with presents. The real reason was that he was informed about the escape of Limahon from Pangasinan. A general and two captains with ten war junks were ordered to escort the fathers safely to Manila, with his own written answer.[63] The purpose of the

---

[63] See the Spanish translation of the letter, dated "3rd year, 7th moon" (1575) of Wanli Emperor", in (in http://www.upf.edu/asia/projectes/che/che16.htm.

fleet was to capture the pirate Limahon who meanwhile had made a fleeting appearance on the China coast, and taken refuge in the Penghu (Pescadores) islands. In fact, on their journey back, the first Europeans reaching Taiwan, the Spaniards were told by fishermen that Limahon had taken refuge there but they did not believe and took no action. Crossing the bay of Amoy, they were shown from the ship deck the place which would be given the Spaniards for a trading-spot, if all went well. The fathers reached Manila on 28 October 1575, without fulfilling their dream to remain in China and preach the Gospel there. Fr. de Rada found a few Christians in Fuzhou, who have received the faith from Portuguese people and was informed that a Portuguese was kept in prison. He brought back a large collection of Chinese books, some of which were subsequently translated at Manila. Unfortunately, most of them have been lost. [64]

The news of the escape of Limahon was confirmed to them in Manila, which gave a blow to their confidence and created a climate of distrust. Moreover, the over five hundred Chinese soldiers who accompanied them were not treated well by the new governor Francisco de Sande (from August 25, 1575, to April 1580) and had to be lodged in private houses of the Spaniards, proving too much for the scanty food supply available. They suffered hardship, and were quite dissatisfied against the new governor, who even refused to provide them with gifts and presents. The Chinese commanders decided to leave on May 4, 1576. Due to the insistence of the governor, they had to take on board Frs. Martin de Rada and Agustin Alburquerque as his ambassadors,[65] but the enterprise turned into a failure,

---

[64] For further details see C.R. Boxer, *South China in the Sixteenth century, o.c.,* p. xlix. "Among the rich things brought, the greatest was that brought by father Martin de Rada, and a thing of great importance and value in those times — namely, a description of the great kingdom of China, its provinces, its boundaries, its religion, its wealth, its civilization, its amusements, and everything that human curiosity is desirous of knowing, of which until then there was no account. This was the account caused to be printed by father Fray Jeronimo Roman, of our order, in the second edition of his *Republicas del Mundo,* which was published by Bishop Fray Pedro [Gonzales] de Mendoza, in his book of that kingdom." (Juan de MEDINA, *Historia de la Orden de S. Augustin de estas Islas Filipinas,* written in 1630, published in Manila in 1893, reported in Blair & Robertson, o.c., vol. 23, p. 239).

[65] The Catalogue of the Augustinians does not provide Fr. Alburquerque's biodata, but relates that he "in several occasions, tried to sell himself as slave in order to reach and preach the Gospel in China".

since the Chinese had no intention of taking the friars back to China without the head of Limahon and some valuable presents. A few days later, the two Augustinians were dumped ashore, and tied up on a tree in a beach at Bolinao (modern Zambales) in North Luzon, by the Chinese soldiers, who also killed other Limahon soldiers, recently taken prisoners, in order to have no witness. The two fathers were liberated few days later by the sergeant major Juan de Morones, who fortunately happened to pass by. Back to the Philippines, De Rada wrote detailed observations on the Chinese people and their way of life and got involved in other cultural concerns.

> *"In the letter [Fr. Rada] wrote to a colleague on 3 June 1576, he gives some idea of his manifold scientific activities. He states that he had compiled* De recta Hidrographiae ratione*', presumably in Latin, and was actively engaged on a* Geometria Practica, *which he was writing in Spanish, 'for it seems to me that nothing has appeared in Spanish on this subject which is worth reading, and it is divided into seven books.' He also intended to write another seven books on 'Cosmography and Astronomy', having already compiled a manuscript work in 'Astrologia Judiciaria', and another on 'all the ways of making clocks.' He complains that he had lost many of his books at sea, and during Limahon's attack on Manila, when the Augustinian convent was burnt; he asks his correspondent to send him mathematical works, 'since I believe that the Lord gave me a special ability and inclination for this, despite my lack of books. For of geometry, Ptolemy and Copernicus; of perspective, Vitelion; of judicial astronomy, Hali-abenragel* [Abu al Asan, a note Spanish-Arab Astrologer]. *I likewise have the book* De Triangulis, *and the 'directions' of Monte Regio* [Regiomontanus, whose real name was Johann Muller, 1436-1476] *and the Ephemerides of Cipriano Leontio* [Cyprian of Leontini, present Lentini in Sicily], *as well as the Alfonsino and Prutenical tables [of the celestial movements].' It is most unfortunate that none of the Rada's scientific works have hitherto come to light, although the possibility remains that one or another of them may be lying forgotten in some Spanish or monastic archive. In any event, it is high time that he was given the credit which is due for being the first European writer on China who clearly and correctly identified this country with Marco Polo's Cathay. Apart from his scientific works, his output in other spheres of knowledge was also considerable. Omitting all mention of the religious and linguistic works which he wrote when in Mexico, we have the titles of two linguistic works which he compiled when in the Philippines, 'Arte y Vocabulario de la lengua Cebuana', and 'Arte e Vocabulario de la lengua China'…"* [66]

------

[66] C.R. Boxer, *South China…*, o.c., Introduction, pp. lxxv-lxxvi. lxxxvii.

In 1578 Fr. de Rada was once again placed on an expedition to Borneo by the governor of Manila, that sailed from Manila on March 3, 1578. It was not successful. On the return voyage many people in the expedition got sick. De Rada was one of them and died at sea on the 12 June 1578.

First Attempt of the Franciscan Friars (1579-1581)

On July 2, 1578, Fr Pedro de Alfaro with 17 other Franciscans of the province of St Joseph, Spain, arrived in Manila (13 priest, 2 lay brothers, and 2 lay choristers). Before 1600, arrived other five new expeditions (8 in 1851, 16 in 1582, 15 in 1583, 12 in 1592 and 16 in 1596), increasing notably their total number, so that it became possible to found the Philippine autonomous province of St Gregory as early as 1586.

On June 15, 1579, the Guardian Pedro de Alfaro, the friars Estevan Ortiz and Agustin de Tordesillas, with three military men, Francisco de Duenas, Juan Diaz Pardo, the Mexican Pedro de Villaroel, a Chinese Juanico and four Filipinos, boarded in Manila a frigate owned by Rodrigo de Frias, and sailed for China, in order to establish a mission. It has been the purpose for their going to the Philippines. Fr. Tordesillas explains: "Our main reason for coming to these parts was to go, if we could, into the great kingdom of China. This desire grew in us daily, because we could see that the Chinese were capable, ingenious and intelligent people, and it would be very easy for them to understand the substance of our Catholic faith…"[67]

The group stopped in North Luzon, where they were joined by two other friars, Frs. Juan Batista Lucarelli of Pesaro and Estevan (of San Francisco) de Baez. At the last-minute Fr. Estevan Ortiz, who spoke Chinese and was to be the interpreter, backed out of the trip because of fear, and remained in North Luzon, causing a lot of worries in everybody and particularly in the Guardian. They departed on June 14, and, by chance, without being intercepted either by pirates or coastguards, they sailed the Xijiang river, and reached the wall of Canton (Guangzhou) on June 21. They wrote to the Bishop Carneiro of Macao informing him of their arrival. He, not trust-

---

[67] See the report in Anastasius Van Den Wyngaert OFM, *Sinica Francescana* (Firenze: Collegium S. Bonaventurae, 1933) vol. II, p. 104.

ing in the good result of the visit, invited them to Macao. They disembarked outside Canton and sang the Te Deum on the river bank. Their arrival caused much consternation to the authorities and among the local populace, who were very curious and diffident. They met with difficulties and cheating by the local Portuguese-speaking resident, Simão, who told the missionaries to be a Christian but who did not properly translate the words of the friars and tried to extort money from them. However, they were fairly treated but they had to be sent from one authority to another. They traveled toward 'Aucheo' (?), and could meet the viceroy or governor of the Two Guangs (Guangdong and Guangxi) in Zhaoqing (from August 20 - September 2) in order to get the permit to remain in China. But they were sent back to Canton, with the permission to stay only for few months and to establish a temporary day-time residence on land, but sleeping on the ship at night. They all fell ill and Fr. Estevan de Baez succumbed. On October 13, Fr. Alfaro wrote to Manila, informing about their present situation, the death of the confrere and the plans of the others.[68]

Fr. Augustin de Tordesillas, with Francesco Duenas and Pardo preferred to return home and were escorted from Canton to 'Chincheo', Fujian (Quanzhou, or the Xiamen Bay), reaching it on December 6, to get a ship bound to Manila. They arrived at the final destination on February 12, 1580, bringing the corpse of Fr. de Baez. The other two fathers, Alfaro and Lucarelli with Villaroel, went to Macau (November 15), welcomed by the bishop and the vicar Andrè Coutinho. They were allowed to establish the convent of Our Lady of the Angels, whose construction started on November 23 and was inaugurate on February 2, 1580. They soon began to accept local novices: young Portuguese joined them, namely Antonio dos Martyres, Boaventura de Lisboa, Rodrigo de Lisboa, Antonio de S. Tomas, and Bernardino de Jesus. Soon after, Fr. Lucarelli built nearby a small chapel dedicated to Our Lady of the Rosary.[69]

---

[68] See "La carta de Frai de Alfaro a Frai Juan de Ayoza Guardián de Nuestra Señora de los Ángeles y Comunes, en Manila su fecha en la ciudad y Río de Cantón a 13 de octubre 1579" in http://www.upf.edu/asia/projectes/che/che16.htm.

[69] For more details see "Viaggio dell'Indie", by Lucarelli and the Report of Tordesillas, in Anastasius Van Den Wyngaert OFM, *Sinica Francescana*, o.c., vol. I, pp. 1-92; see also Manuel Texeira, "Os Franciscanos em Macau", in *Archivio Ibero-Americano*, 1978, nos. 149-152. Pablo de Jesus (1533-1610, custodian of the Philippines province in July 1,

Although the Portuguese civil and religious authorities initially welcomed the newcomers, they soon became concerned that their monopoly in the relationship with China might be threatened by a significant number of Franciscans, especially if Spanish, present in Macao. So, Fr. Alfaro, falsely accused of misconduct, was ordered to report to the authorities in Goa and in the following June had to leave Macau, meeting with death in a storm during the journey. Fr. Lucarelli, being Italian, was put in charge of the convent. Late in 1581, always due to the opposition of the Portuguese, he also was forced to go to Malacca, together with Fr. Anthony de S. Tomas and Boaventura de Lisboa, leaving Bernardino de Jesus with some novices. He was welcomed by the bishop of Malacca, Mgr. Joao Ribeiro Gaio, who asked him to found the convent and the church of St. Joseph. Not long after, in 1582, the Captain Aires Gonçalves de Miranda, coming from India, invited him to return to Macau. The trip took two months and they arrived in August and the friar continued to work in the convent, gathering people from different races and studying Chinese. He tried to enter China, but was always impeded by the Portuguese merchants.

Development of the Jesuit presence in Macao (1565-1582)

In 1565, we have already seen, the Jesuits opened their first house in Macau. Fr. Texiera wrote in 1568: "In our port in China where we have been established, a church and a house were built for the Society. There are about five or six thousand Christian souls there, that is, some Portuguese who live there as well as other Christians."[70]

On 15 August 1567, the Spanish Jesuit Juan Bautista de Ribera (1525-1594) with Pedro Bonaventure Riera (1526-1573) reached Macao and, from there, he proceeded to Canton, arriving on 9 May 1568. Fr. Ribera, tried to go night time to Nan'ao, but was soon taken by the boat owner back to Macau. He felt hopeless in converting Chinese people in peaceful ways. Sometime before October 1568, Fr. Pedro Bonaventura Riera made his try and went to Canton with some Portuguese merchants.

1580) described this mission to Pope Gregory XIII, in a letter dated 14 July 1580, reported in Blair & Robertson, *The Philippines Islands,* o.c., vol. 34, pp. 321-322.

[70] Letter, quoted in Videira Pires, *The Genesis of St. Paul's College* (Macau 1954), p. 7.

In June 1568, Bishop Melchior Carneiro (1519-1583), himself a Jesuit, who was appointed in 1555 the second coadjutor of the Patriarch of Ethiopia, arrived in Macau to care for the evangelization of China and Japan and in 1569 went and spent some time in Canton.

The number of the Jesuits in Macao gradually grew. Fr. Soldi Gnecchi Organtino, who was in charge of the community, writing in 1570, reported the name of those who lived with him: Frs. Boaventura Riera, Gonçalo de Cunha, Baltasar Lopes, Diego de Mesquita, Francisco Cabral and Bro. Andrè Pinto.

In 1572, the Visitor, Fr. Gonçalo Alvares, opened a primary school annexed to the residence, in which Latin class was added in 1575.

In 1574, Fr. Antonio Vaz (1523-1573?) was in Canton from 7 February to about 20 March.

In 1575, Fr. Cristovão da Costa (1529-1581) accompanied Portuguese merchants to Canton twice and stayed there on one occasion for two months and on another occasion for a month, but could not obtain permission to remain. He made friend with a 20-year young man, disciple of a Buddhist monk, who later followed him to Macau and study the Catholic doctrine. After his baptism as Paul on December 25, 1575, the Buddhist monk raised the anger of Canton people who threatened to destroy Portuguese ships and goods. The Portuguese at Canton for the 1576 fair, promised to hand back the young man. The latter was entrusted to Bishop Carneiro [71] who took him to Canton and handed him back, witnessing to his beatings.

Fr. Juan B. Ribera tried again to settle in Canton in 1575.

Fr. Cristovão da Costa, who was in charge in 1576 reported to the Jesuit General, Everardo Mercuriano, that the residence at Macao was a busy place and beside the regular staff there were 14 Jesuits who were on their way to Japan. Seven of these had already been ordained, three were studying theology, two were studying Latin and other two were temporary coadjutors. [72] There were about 150 children attending school.

---

[71] He died in Macau on august 19, 1583, after having founded two hospitals for the poor, and the Casa da Misericordia. In a letter dated November 1562, from Macao, he described his hope to open a mission in China.

[72] Videira Pires, *The Genesis of St. Paul's College*, o.c., p. 7.

In 1578, Fr. Mateo Lopez informed that they were usually five fathers and more brothers, engaged in prayer, confessions, teaching children to read, write, and sing. The residents in Macao were about ten thousand among Christians and pagans, with five churches. The concern of the fathers was restricted to teaching and to the service to the Portuguese community, while their interest for China was limited. Some of the priests used to accompany the Portuguese merchants to Canton and celebrated Mass for them in a Buddhist temple, on Shamien island, where the ships used to anchor. Fr. Alessandro Valignano, the Visitor of the Missions of the Indies,[73] as soon as he arrived to Macao in September 1578, realized that none of the missionaries stationed there, although visiting Canton with Portuguese merchants, has succeeded in establishing positive and lasting contacts with China. To make evangelical headway into China, missionaries needed a deep knowledge of the local language and culture, and also to adapt themselves to the local living conditions. To this end, he wrote to the Superior in India, Fr. Vincent Ruiz, asking him to send to Macau a person who would be equal to the task, namely Bernardino de Ferraris (1537-1584). However, as Fr. de Ferraris was busy as the new rector at Cochin, Fr. Michele Ruggieri (1543-1607), was sent to Macau.

Valignano saw a new building finished in February 1579 on the nearby hill (the hill where now stand the ruins of St. Paul's Church). He left Macau for Japan on 7 July 1579, leaving behind instructions for Ruggieri, who was to arrive within days. In fact, the Italian Jesuit reached Macao on 20 July 1579. He soon started to study the Chinese language. For Easter 1580 (3 April), he went to Canton, and stayed in a house near the river. In the same year, Fr. Ruggieri started in Macau a class for Chinese catechumens, the St. Martin's house, on the same hill in a second building thanks to the sum of 300 escudos given by an Italian who joined the Franciscan Order.

In 1581, there were in Macau Frs. Pedro Gomez, Visitor from India, Domenico Alvarez, rector of the house, Fernando Martinez, André Pinto,

---

[73] Fr. Alessandro Valignano (1539-1606): in 1572 he was appointed Visitor of the Mission from India to Japan and reached Goa in 1574 with 41 confreres. After visiting the Missions in India and Malacca, he arrived at Macao on September 6, 1578 remaining until July 7, 1579, leaving for Japan with Frs. Pedro Gomez, Alvaro Diaz, Gustavão Moreira and Francisco Pirez.

Michele Ruggieri and Bro. Antonio Paez. In the same year, Fr. Ruggieri returned twice to Canton, accompanied alternatively by Fr. André Pinto and Bro. Paez. He remained the first time for three months, the second time for two months, being housed in the palace of the Siamese ambassador, where he could arrange a room as a chapel, dedicated to Our Lady: the Portuguese during their stay in Canton went there for the Sunday Mass.

On March 9, 1582, Fr. Valignano returned to Macao from Japan, accompanying four young noble Japanese on their way to Portugal and to Rome, [74] and remained until the end of December. The Jesuit church and residence were transferred to new building, while the class for catechumens of Fr. Ruggieri provided also classes in Portuguese and Latin languages. Late in 1582 there were in Macau 25 Jesuits, among whom Bishop Carneiro, 17 priests and seven scholastics.

Meanwhile, in mid-April 1582, Ruggieri had gone to Canton for the fourth time, staying in the place of the Siamese ambassador. There, as we will see in greater details, on May 2, he could be joined by the confreres Fr. Alonso Sanchez (1551-1614), Bro. Gallardo and two Franciscans, from the Philippines: "In this house – wrote Fr. Sanchez - the father was staying when I went to China for the first time and in it with him the mandarins put me up, and there, several times, we could celebrate Mass..." [75]

---

[74] "At the beginning of 1582, Valignano left Japan and went to India. His journey had a double purpose; firstly to see that the affairs in India were prospering, and secondly to head a delegation of Japanese Princes, who were to visit the Pope and the King, and by their presence, excite the interest of Rome and Lisbon in their distant country. The last plan was a bold and far-sighted one, and Valignano was long responsible for its design and execution. The journey was long and dangerous, so they chose four of the youngest members of each of the three Christian princely houses of Daimyos from Kiu-Siu. On February 20, 1582, the young men, with a small suite, accompanied the Visitor, sailed on to the ship, which belonged to Ignacio de Lima. Twenty days later they were all comfortably quartered in the Jesuit College of Macao. They were to study Latin there under Farther Diego de Mesquita, until nine months period of waiting had elapsed and they could continue their journey to India. At last December 31st arrived, the date fixed for their departure." (Felix A. Plattner, *Jesuits Go East*, Westminster, Maryland, The Newman Press, 1952, pp. 92-93).

[75] See Spanish text of Sanchez's report of his second trip to China, Macao 1585, (in http://www.upf.edu/asia/ projectes/che/che16.htm): *En esta casa estava el padre quando yo fuí la primera vez a la China y en ella y con él me pusieron a mi los mandarines y dixe muchas veces misa...*

Jesuit and Franciscan Attempts

Why could this meeting happen? It was occasioned by two contemporary attempts from Manila, one by the Franciscans and the second by the Jesuit Alonso Sanchez, that became interrelated.

In this same year 1582, in fact, another group of Franciscans took the initiative. About 20 of them, led by the Visitor Commissar Jeronimo de Burgos (+1593), had reached the Philippines from Spain through Mexico in February 1582. Seven friars were assigned to China: Pablo de Jesus (1533-1610, who has become Guardian in the Philippines at the departure of Pedro de Alfaro in 1579, and will become *praepositus* (superior) of the newly established St. Gregory province in 1591), Martin Ignacio de Loyola (+1612), Jerome de Aguilar (+1591), Agustin de Tordesillas (the same who took part of the first trip to China), Antonio de Villanova (c. 1520-1582), as well as the lay brothers Francisco de Cordova, and Cristoval Gomez, the ship pilot. Together with three soldiers, among whom again Juan Diaz Pardo (for the second time), and six Filipino natives, they tried to enter China when the Visitor, Fray Jeronimo de Burgos, organized an expedition without the government approval. They left Manila for Macau at the beginning of March 1582, led by Fr. Pablo de Jesus. They did not reach their destination, however, since a typhoon blew them back towards the coast of Pangasinan.

In the meantime, on March 14, the Governor Gonzalo Ronquillo de Peñalosa had sent the Jesuit Fr. Alonso Sanchez, as his ambassador to solicit the acceptance of Philip II as king of both Spain and Portugal from Macau residents. He has given the message to the *Alcalde Mayor* (administrative and judicial head) of the province of Pangasinan, to reach the Franciscan group and not let them continue the journey, except for the Guardian and anyone Fr. Sanchez would accept. The friars were intercepted by the official and gave up the trip: Pablo de Jesus left other two going with the Jesuit father, Juan Díaz Pardo and/or Juan Pobre (Juan the Poor [76]).

---

[76] According to Manuel Texeira (a.c.), they are two different persons, while according to other writers Juan Pobre is the nickname of Juan Dias Pardo, and the other Franciscan remained unknown.

Before leaving Manila, for his trip to China, Fr. Sanchez had taken the precaution of asking Governor to accredit him as an ambassador and he carried a sealed credential to this effect, written in Chinese, together with a letter stating that he had a message from the Governor of the Philippines for the Viceroy of Guangdong.

Fr. Sanchez and Bro. Gallardo with the two Franciscans, who increased to 26 the number of his entourage, among whom a Bengal native baptized Alonso as interpreter and Juan Baptista Barragán, sailed for China. They met a storm and reached the port of Jicshi, Shanwei district, Guangdong, on April 6. Sanchez was taken to see the admiral and forced, against his will, to kneel down and stay in that position for two hours. But, when Sanchez showed the documents to the local admiral, they were acknowledged and the party was treated reasonably well. Sanchez and his party were escorted to "Lampo", probably Nan'ao Island, the headquarters of the naval commander. Then, they were taken by inland on foot to Hoi Fung City and waterway to Huizhou, where the ship's crew and servants, including Alonso Gomez and Bautista Barragan, had to remain while Sanchez and the friars were taken to Canton, on May 2.

"When the missionaries disembarked on the outskirts of the city, the commander of their escort intimated to them for a consideration of silver, that he would take them to where they could meet other foreigners. They had no money on them, but promised the officer he would be paid if he fulfilled his part of the bargain. They were then led very secretly through the back streets to where some Portuguese ships lay at anchor…. Sanchez's group was summoned to appear before a magistrate, but while their case was being determined, an imperial commissioner arrived, which meant the suspension of all official business for three days. When he eventually reappeared before the magistrate, Sanchez was granted a safe-conduct to Macau, but this has to be ratified by the viceroy in Zhaoqing. Meanwhile, the viceroy was enquiring into the status of Macau and the Portuguese right to be there at all. He heard of the presence of Sanchez's party, and when he asked about them, one of his officials, who had picked up on Iberian jealousies, told him that, as Spaniards, these missionaries were of the meaner sort, 'thieves and spies who had come to learn the language, and find out the country's harbors… a bad race who went about snatching others' kingdoms… and who carried off everything from whatever lands they took over'… Sanchez's party was ordered to be further detained, and the viceroy demanded that an official come from Macau to explain its status, the justification for the Portuguese presence and their assumed right to build houses, churches, and fortifications there, as well as the nature of their relations with the Spaniards.

The *capitan mor* (Major Captain) of Macau, Juan de Almeida asked Mathias Panela, a judicial auditor of Macau, to go to Zhaoqing as his representative, along with Fr. Michele Ruggieri, appointed by Fr. Valignano as representative of the bishop. Ruggieri was then in Canton and received the letter from Fr. Valignano. Fr. Sanchez, who has been taken to the place in Canton where Fr. Ruggieri was and stay, talked with him about his situation. Ruggieri and Panela went to Zhaoqing and succeeded to gain the favor of the Viceroy [Chen Rui] for Macau. Ruggieri asked the permission to stay in China in order to learn the Chinese culture and pleaded for the case of Fr. Sanchez, giving his personal guarantee for his good behavior. It was Holy Trinity Sunday, when they got the positive answer (the *chapa*, or license, was dated May 14). They went back to Canton to bring it to Fr. Sanchez, who therefore could leave Canton on May 29. He reached Macau and stayed in the Jesuit house.

After soliciting from the Macau Portuguese the oath of allegiance to Philip II, Sanchez left the port on July 6, 1582 aboard of a *nau*, the gross carrack of the yearly trade, taking some two hundred and eighty people to Japan and then to the Philippines. Juan Pobre was invited by a Portuguese friend to follow the *nau* on a lighter boat and go to Japan. However, the *nau* ran into a storm and was wrecked off the coast of Taiwan on July 16 while the small boat could continue and reach Japan. The stranded travelers lived on the Taiwan shore for more almost three months in tents attacked and ill-treated by local people. They could survive with just a little rice. Then, with a makeshift boat they left and returned to Macao, on October 4.

---

[77] Gregory James (ed.) *Through Spanish Eyes* (Hong Kong: Hong Kong University of Science and Technology, 2003): Introduction, pp. xxix-xxx, quoting also from the *Journals* of Fr. Ricci.

90

"We all left the ship however we could, some floating on planks, other swimming, but a few were drowned when the great junk broke up, and all the cargo was scattered and rotted on the beach. The natives soon appeared, naked, with bows and quivers; with great boldness and determination, they broke into our camp, and… without wounding anyone, they stole much of what we had been able to salvage from the wreck. This happened until we had dried out and could defend ourselves. They came around day and night, attacking us with their arrows, killing some and wounding many. We lived like this for more than three months, with just a little rice, which we were able to dry, until we managed to put together a small boat from the pieces of the wrecked ship. Over 290 of us embarked, with no ballast nor provision, and with only five or six jars of water and a little rice… Once we set off, God gave us such a wind that after seven or eight days we returned to Macau…"[78]

---

[78] Sanchez: *Relación breve de la jornada quel P. Alonso Sánchez déla Compañía deJesús hizo por harden y parezer del Sr. D. Gonzalo Ronquillo de Peñalosa, governador de Philipinas, y del Sr. obispo y oficiales de S. M. desde la Isla de Luzón y ciudad de Manila a los Reynos de la China*. See also José Eugenio Borao, *Primer documento occidental sobre Taiwan: La narración del naufragio del jesuita Pedro Gómez, en la costa de Taiwan el 16 de julio de 1582*, Sinapia, no. 8, 1996, First Semester, pp. 106-111: "The first documented Christian activity that occurred in Taiwan came about through an accident. It dates back to the period of exploration at the end of the sixteenth century. The source of information was eyewitness reports of the missionaries and their descriptions of the oriental milieu. It was a actually fortuitous coming. In 1582 a Portuguese ship sank on its way to Japan. The survivors stayed on the island of Taiwan for two months until they managed to build a smaller boat from the wreckage of the old one, and eventually returned to Macao. Four Jesuit priests - two of whom were Spaniards (Alonso Sánchez and Pedro Gómez) and two who were Portuguese (Cristobal Moreira and Alvaro de Toro) - boarded the ship, thus spearheading the first Christian activity on Taiwan. Pedro Gómez wrote an exhaustive letter that was published in 1597. His letter was included in a collection of letters written by the Jesuits and published in Portugal for propagandist motives either within the Order itself or among their readers in Europe. The letter of Gómez gave an account of the Masses, processions, and veneration of a "relic" of St. Ursula that Gómez had brought for Japan. The group of nearly three hundred survivors, which consisted of Chinese, Japanese, and Portuguese was on "stopover" in Taiwan. Moreover, their attempted contact with the natives, trading objects and wood from the boat for sacks of rice lasted only briefly because of the growing suspicion among the natives. "This lasted a few days because the natives were so scandalized by the confusion that happened, that they no longer brought us aid as friends, but shot arrows at us and spied on us like enemies." Consequently, there was no attempt at all to establish missionary contact with the natives."

In Macau, meanwhile, since March Fr. Valignano with the Japanese princes was living there and in August Frs. Matteo Ricci and Pasio also arrived. Fr. Sanchez could meet and share views with them.

In December, Juan Pobre and his small ship could return to Macau, together with Gonzalo Garcia, a former Jesuit postulant and a future martyr, who was attracted by the wonderful example of Juan's poor life. Fr. Sanchez asked him a lot of information about the Jesuits in Japan and their evangelization method; consequently, he wrote a report to the Superior General in Rome, as well as a letter to the confreres in Japan, raising his critiques about their work and method. Fr. Valignano felt unhappy about it.

Meanwhile, the crew and the ship, which brought Fr. Sanchez from Manila, were kept like prisoners still in Nan'ao and Huizhou since April; it was only after five months with the help of Matias Panela [79] and the interpreter Alonso of Bengal that they were released and sent to Macau.

Further attempts of the Franciscans

The above-mentioned Franciscan friars who could not continue their trip to China went back to Manila. After a long discussion with the governor and the bishop, they obtained the permit to embark for China once more, from Cavite. So, with the necessary licenses, the group of 26 members (among whom the religious, Martin Ignacio de Loyola, Agustin de Tordesilhas, Jeronimo de Aguilar, Antonio de Villanova, who arrived to Manila form Mexico the previous year), two lay brothers Francisco de Cordova (de Gata) and Cristobal Gomez under religious habit, and the soldier

---

This article contains the Spanish translation of Pedro Gómez's letter that was published in the collection *Cartas que os Padres e Irmaos da Companhia de Iesus escrevarao dos Reynos de Japao & China aos damesma Compania da India & Europa desde anno de 1549 ate o de 1580* (Letters written by the Priests of the Company of Jesus to the Two Kingdoms of Japan and China, and to India and Europe from 1549 to 1580), vol. I, Em Evora, by Manuel de Lyra, MDXCVII. An original copy of this book may be found in the Rare Books Section of the National Library of Taiwan.

[79] Panela > Gov. G. Ronquillo, February 10, 1583, from Macau: he stated that he has helped Fr. Sanchez's companions to get their ship 'six leagues from Macau', as well as Fr. Jeronimo de Burgos and the other Franciscans out of prison, as we'll see.

Juan de Feria, owner of the ship) left on June 21, 1582, with Fray Jeronimo de Burgos as their leader. However, they did not land at Macau, as they had intended, but at Zhelin, near Chaozhou, in North Guangdong[80], where they were thrown into jail by the Chinese authorities, since they were considered robbers. Then, they were sent to Canton, via Huizhou, and condemned to death. Fortunately, they were ransomed by the Macau's Captain Major Aires Gonzales de Mirandas, who sent to Canton the Portuguese official Matias Panela, to plead for their case. Fr. Antonio de Villanova, however, died in captivity. They were liberated and sent to Macau in August 1582. [81]

In Macau, Fr. de Burgos was advised to establish a new autonomous Province (Custodia) with the two convents of Macao and Malacca, choosing Fr. Martin Ignacio as first Provincial (*Custos*) with Fr. Jeronimo d'Aguillar Guardian of the Macau convent having Frs. Tordesilhas and Cordova under him, while Fr. Lucarelli Guardian of the convent of Malacca. Fr. Martin Ignacio de Loyola left on 27 December 1582, with Fr. John B. Lucarelli, followed on December 31 by the ship with Fr. Valignano and the Japanese Princes, returning to Malacca, via Hainan, where they arrived in January 27, 1583. [82] Fr. Tordesilhas and Juan Pobre left for Siam, but, due to the illness, returned to Macau after about two months.

On February 13, 1583, Fr. Sanchez, with 26 members of his crew (among whom Cristoval Gomez and Juan de Feria) and Jeronimo de Burgos with his 17 Franciscan party, left again Macao on the ship of Bartolomeu Vaz (Baez) Landeiro, piloted by Sebastiâo Jorge, and reached Manila on March 27.

Back to Manila, Fr. de Burgos discussed with the Guardian of the Franciscan province of St Gregory, Pablo de Jesus, another missionary expedition to Cochinchina (present North Vietnam). So, on May 4, 1583, eight Franciscan missionaries departed for Cochinchina: they were Frs. Diego de

---

⁸⁰ Some sources speak about Fujian.

⁸¹ See Anastasius Van Den Wyngaert OFM, *Sinica Francescana*, o.c., vol. II, pp. 210-213.

⁸² Then, together they went to Cochin and Goa (India). Fr. Martin Ignacio reached Lisboa in August 1584. He wrote his 'Itinerary'. Fr. Lucarelli in 1585, went back to Italy, via Portugal. He died in St Lucy Convent, Naples in 1604. He wrote his report in "Viaggio dell'Indie", which has been republished in *Sinica Francescana*, o.c., vol. II.

Oropesa (or de S. José, +1590) the leader, Bartholome Ruiz (c.1500-1600), Francisco de Montilla (+1603), Pedro Ortiz Cabezas, and three lay brothers Diego Jimenez, Francisco Villorino, Cristoval Gomez, the ship pilot, and a novice, Manuel de Santiago (de St. James +1625), accompanied by three Filipino servant boys. [83]

Fr. de Burgos was required to return to Europe to explain the reasons for his establishing an autonomous province. So, on June 15, 1583, he sailed for Mexico on the ship St. Juan, together with some people from Perú. Unfortunately, as we will see, then ship met with a strange fate.

The trip of the Cochinchina expedition was fine, but the welcome was not, at their reaching the bay of Da Nang on May 22. But soon the mood of local people changed: after the celebration of the Eucharist, they were summoned by the local king and sent away. While on the way, a storm blew them to the Hainan Island. Here they were chained and as prisoners were taken first to Changhua, then to Qiongzhou, where they were helped by a Chinese merchant from Zhangzhou and a negro (a former slave of Portuguese of Macau). On July 27, they left the island of Hainan for Leizhou, Wuzhou, Zhaoqing, on August 19, where the viceroy sent them all by boat to Canton (arriving there on August 22).

Fr. Diego de Oropesa wrote:

"We then left Zhaoqing on to Canton, which is about 24 leagues down river from there and we made it in two days. The Chinese who were accompanying us landed, but told us to wait in the boat. While we were waiting, a Portuguese-speaking Chinese came up and told us that in the Siamese cantonment (which is where foreigners are lodged) there were two fathers. We understood that they were Jesuits who had come from Macao. I was extremely pleased at this, and immediately wrote them a note, and asked the native to go with our interpreter and deliver it. We waited for a long time, and when they didn't return with the reply, the lay sailor who had come with us [Cristoval Gomez] went there. It was God's will that without knowing the way through those streets, he chanced not on the Jesuits fathers but a friar

---

[83] About this expedition, see the details and the reports in Gregory James (ed.) *Through Spanish Eyes* (Hong Kong: Hong Kong University of Science and Technology, 2003): the Account of Diego de Oropesa (pp. 221-323). About Fray Francisco de Montilla, in particular, it reports the accounts written by Ivan de Santa Maria, *Chronica de la Provincia de San Joseph de los Descalços de la Orden de los Menores de nuestro Seraphico Padre S. Francisco* (Madrid: Imprenta Real, 1615).

of our own Order [Jeronimo de Burgos], together with a cleric and another gentleman from Peru, who'd arrived there three days previously through a strange series of events, which went like this. On 15th June of the same year, 1583, a carrack called San Juan left Manila for New Spain, and taking a slightly different route from her usual one, two days after St. John's Day [June 26] ran into such rough weather (although they were keeping close to the island of Luzon) that they were almost lost at sea. But for the great glory of God, they were almost miraculously saved, and running with the storm they fetched up on the coast of China at a port called Lam'ao [Nam'ao] which is about sixty leagues from Canton, towards the north, near Chincheo. There were some passengers on the ship and two of our friars, who were taking messages from the Guardian to His Majesty concerning matters relating to the welfare of the country and our custody. There was another old friar, called Fray Juan de Contreras, who'd come from Peru, and two gentlemen who'd come with him, and two Augustinians and a cleric. As the carrack approached land, some warships came out to meet it, because there is a fleet [stationed] in that large port. The commander of those ships told some of them to accompany him on land to speak to his general. One of the friars of our Order, called Fray Geronimo de Burgos, who'd already been in China the year before, together with a cleric, one of the Peruvian gentlemen, called Juan de Mendoça, and two negroes jumped into the boat with the captain. When they reached the land, they went to speak with the captain-major of that fleet, called the chum pin *(which is their name for the admiral,* zhong bing*), who gave them a good reception and ordered the carrack to stay there until an order came from the viceroy and those who'd already landed had gone to negotiate with him. For this he gave them people to accompany them, and sent them to another senior mandarin, who lives in the city of Sancheo [?] which is one of the biggest and best in China. From there they were taken to the viceroy, who referred them to the* haidao, *as he had done with us…*

When they saw our sailor, and he them, they were all amazed and didn't know what to say to each other, because it seemed like a dream. They wrote a letter in which they told me all about their problem. They advised me to be very careful with our case so that the Chinese wouldn't realize that we were all from the same place, because they might think that we were all spies, who had come by different routes…

At this point our companions came and took us to the haidao, *who, without seeing us, referred us to the* quan chim fu (guangshifu)*… He treated us humanely and smilingly got up and ordered us to get up too and carried on speaking to us for a long time. He asked if we knew Fray Geronimo and Don Juan de Mendoça. We said we didn't…*

The next day, which is St. Bartholomew's Day (24 August), the quan chim fu *sent for Fray Geronimo and his companions and gave them papers to allow them to go to Macao and send for their carrack from there. We however stayed in that prison, very sad and forgotten by men… There we stayed for 22 days, in great perplexity… In the middle of all this trouble there arrived, on the eve of the Feast of the Nativity of Our Lady, two Italian Jesuits, one called Miguel Rogerio [Michele Ruggieri], and the other Thomas Ricio [Matteo Ricci]. Miguel Rogerio knows a great deal about Chinese language, especially the writing. They had been invited by the viceroy to take over a house in Zhaoqing to settle there to become residents of the glorious Kingdom of China, as they call it….*

The joy, their arrival gave us, was beyond words. They were with us on the day of our Lady [September 8]… They promised us that when they go to Zhaoqing they would negotiate our freedom with the viceroy, and would send us the papers for us to go to Macao without anyone troubling us. When our merchant saw the Fathers were going to Zhaoqing and they'd certainly be sending us the papers to enable us to leave there, and he himself was in danger of having his dubious dealings brought to light (also because the fathers would be seen to be the main agents of our freedom and to be more deserving our gratitude), he worked so hard on our case that the following Saturday the quan chim fu *summoned us and gave us the papers to go to Macao… We make haste and left Canton on Sunday morning, arriving in Macao on the next day, which was 16ᵗʰ September… where we were received by our brothers with great joy and satisfaction. Those in Macao were quite unprepared for our arrival because, although Fray Geronimo Burgos has said we were there and made great efforts [on our behalf] and I also had written to the bishop and to other people, the case was progressing so slowly….'*[84]

The Jesuits Frs. Ruggieri and Ricci, as we will see in detail, had arrived from Macao on September 7. The group met them in their place, but the Jesuits could just console them and promise to help, but nothing more, because of the prompt initiative of the Chinese merchant.[85]

It was September 15 when the Franciscans left Canton, and they arrived

---

[84] Diego de Oropesa's manuscript, *Itinerarium Discalceatorum Manilae*, in Gregory James, *Through Spanish Eyes*, o. c. pp. 311-321.

[85] The Jesuit interpretation reads: "Since our Fathers were at liberty, they were permitted to treat the captives with kindness and courtesy… and the happy meeting finally resulted in the deliverance of the whole party…Our fathers promised that whatever was demanded of the prisoners would be paid with interest from Macao, and in a short time, after they distributed their belonging to the poor, the captives were dispatched to Macao…" (Ricci, Journals, II.4.146-147, Louis J. Gallegher, *China in the Sixteenth century: The Journals of Matthew Ricci: 1583-1610*, New York: Random House, 1953).

to Macau on the following day, welcomed by their confreres in the convent whose guardian was Fr. Agustin de Tordesillas who had come back from Siam where he went with Bro. Juan Pobre, as well as by the bishop and the Jesuits. Benefactors paid the Chinese merchant, owner of the ship, all the expenses he claimed.

The successful attempt of the Jesuits from Macau [86]

In the mid of 1582, after having met the viceroy Chen Rui and pleaded for the permit for Fr. Sanchez, Fr. Ruggieri and Panela returned to Macau to report the results of the embassy, with some money of the viceroy to buy other goods for him. Later, however, when the viceroy, captivated by the courtesy of Fr. Ruggieri and out of the desire to obtain the gifts bought in Macao and the clock promised by the father, invited him with the official letter and permit, to establish a church in Zhaoqing, Ruggieri due to a sickness could not go and send the presents through Panela. At the renewal of the invitation from the viceroy, Valignano still in Macao, decided to send back Ruggieri together with Francisco Pasio (1554-1612, who had arrived from India with Matteo Ricci on August 7, 1582). They left Macau on December 18, 1582, together with Bro. Baltasar y Gonzalo and the Chinese Christian Felipe Mendes as interpreter, reaching Zhaoqing on December 27. They were given a Buddhist pagoda to stay in and to open a church and a residence. The viceroy paid them a visit of courtesy and asked them to shave and to wear the robe of Buddhist monks. They also got the permit for Fr. Ricci and Bro. Diego to reside in China (February 5, 1583). But unfortunately, their stay did not last long due to the fall into disgrace and the removal of the viceroy Chen Rui (in mid-February). They have to return to Macao, probably in March 1583 (although Ricci writes 'after four or five months') with a sealed document of the viceroy to the vice-commissioner of Guangzhou to allow them to have a residence and a church in the city.

---

[86] For more details, see P. D'Elia, *Fonte Ricciane*, o.c., v. I, nos. 211-237; Fernando Bortone, *P. Matteo Ricci, il Saggio d'Occidente* (Roma: Desclée. 1965); Edward Malatesta, "Alessandro Valignano, Fan Li-an (1539-1606) Strategist of the Jesuit Mission in China, in The Jesuits 1594-1994", in *Review of Culture* (Istituto Cultural de Macau, 1994).

However, they were not even allowed to land at Canton. However, the document with the permit turned out to be very important, since the Canton authorities wanted it back. Ruggieri insisted to hand it personally to them, and, since by this time Pasio had gone on to Japan (left Macao on July 24 together with other Jesuits), after consultation with the new superior Fr. Francisco Capral, he brought Fr. Matteo Ricci with him, who after his arrival immediately started to study Chinese and to take care of the center for catechumens, St. Martin house. After some adventures with the authorities in Xiangshang and even with the *haidao* in Canton, during a very short visit, due to their refusal to hand the letter to a messenger from Canton, they finally succeeded to return to Guangzhou on September 7. Ricci recorded:

"Both times [the fathers reached Canton], *they met in the provincial capital some Spaniards from the Philippines. The first time, they were three persons, who, sailing in a ship from the Philippines to New Spain [Mexico], were thrown by the storm on a coast of the Guangdong, called Namtao [it should be Nan'ao], where they succeeded to gain the shore and the three of them had come [to the capital] on behalf of their companions to explain the reason of their presence to the Tutang and Haidao, and to ask the permit to take refuge in Macau in order to repair their ship.*

This second time, they found in the city eight or ten members of the Franciscan Order, who had voyaged also from the Philippines to the kingdom of Cochinchina. They had heard that the king of that country wanted to build a Christian church and some priests. But they were not well treated and so they returned to their land. Due to a strong storm, they were shipwrecked to the island of Hainan, where they were caught by the Chinese soldiers, robbed of whatever they possessed, and brought to Guangdong to the officials, accused as pirates. Great was the consolation for them and for the Fathers to see all together united by the same cause in the midst of pagans. Therefore, the Fathers showed them all the kindness, and help them to attend and celebrate Mass in the chapel the Father kept in the palace of the Siam ambassadors. They were consoled for it, but even more for the good advice they gave to the Chinese to treat them well, since in Macau they would repay for everything will be spent on them…"[87]

---

[87] D'Elia, *Fonti Ricciane*, o.c., I, 233, pp. 179-180.

In the meantime, a guard of the new viceroy Guo had submitted him a petition to allow the 'foreign bonzes' to have a residence. At last, the petition was accepted. The two fathers could reach Zhaoqing. The local prefect (cifu, named Guangpuon, Wang Pan) welcomed them and later allowed them to buy a piece of land, to build a residence and a church. The presence of the Jesuits became permanent: it was September 10, 1583.

Sanchez's second trip to Macau (1584-1585)

The concern for China in the Philippines continued to be high. Exchange of letters from Frs. Ruggieri, Pasio and Ricci to the Bishop, the Governor and Fr. Sanchez in Manila, asking also for financial support for their mission, as we will see in detail, increased especially in the later the desire to return to China. Fr Sanchez suggested to the other authorities in Manila to propose through the Italian Jesuit friends an official Spanish embassy to the Chinese Emperor.

The good occasion for a second journey was offered by the 'mutiny' of the St. Juan galleon, which had left Manila for Mexico on June 15, 1583, with Fr. Jeronimo de Burgos and others on board, as we have seen, in order to bring the news of the death of the Governor Ronquillo and of the big fire in Manila during his funeral: on the contrary, it has been deviated to China and to Macau, where it was intended to be loaded with goods for Perú. The news was brought to Manila in March 1584 by a merchant of Macau, Bartolomeo Vaz Landeiro, who had provided two junks to the captain of the galleon and to those who did not support the mutiny.

The *Real Fator* (Royal Factor or Exactor) Juan Baptista Roman and Fr. Sanchez left Manila towards the end of April, and after a very fast journey, they entered the port of Macao on May 1, led by Chinese coast guards.

Roman, after meeting the local both civil and religious authorities, dealt with the mutineers, punishing the most responsible people, especially Juan de Mendoça, to whom was attributed the initiative since he had come from Perú. Then, he sent the galleon with its passengers back to its proper direction, Mexico. Meanwhile, Fr. Sanchez dealt with the embassy affair with the Italian Jesuits, writing to them about the plan, as we will see in details in the next chapter.

Roman and Sanchez, however, could not go to Zhaoqing and meet the viceroy, as desired. In August or early September, they could meet Fr. Ruggieri, who was sent to Macau to collect funds and other necessities, since according to Ricci, "they were with many debts and without money".[88] He handed them the report of Fr. Ricci, and received from them money and gifts brought from Manila. Then, on October 1, after being allowed to load the ship with merchandise, they left Macau, and after some misfortunes, that brought them to Hainan and Malacca (stopping there 3-4 months), arrived in Manila on June 6, 1585: with them, there were another Jesuit, and ten Franciscans, two from Macao and the others from Malacca, among whom Diego de Oropesa and Francisco de Montilla.

Further attempts of members of other Congregations

Ricci wrote:

"Later on, also many religious members of St. Francis, St. Dominic and St. Augustine left Europe in order to reach this part of the world and get fruits in this kingdom, mainly via New Spain [Mexico] and the Philippines, although they could not remain within it, and most of them returned to the Philippines, while some of them stayed over in Macao."[89]

This was against the official policy of the Spanish government and the Manila authorities. In fact, the first part of the tenth chapter of the Memorial of the 1586 *Audencia* in Manila provides "the information about the disorders created by the religious who leave the islands for other countries without orders from the governor or bishop". It continues describing the damage caused by the departures of these religious: "they declare, as soon as they arrive here, that they do not come to the islands, but for China; and therefore they do not give themselves to the language of the Indians, or intercourse with them - but rather, to give color to their own acts in traveling farther to satisfy their curiosity and see new lands,

---

[88] P. D'Elia, *Fonti Ricciane*, o.c., I, no, 255, p. 201. Ricci does not mention any other motivation.

[89] P. D'Elia, *Fonti Ricciane*, o.c., I, no. 287, p. 232)

they speak evil of the natives and of the country, thus giving a bad name, in speech and by letter…".

About "the wrongs committed in the countries where the religious and the seculars go without orders", it stated: "The injuries on the part of the countries whither they go are no less, because those people are all disturbed and offended, and consider the religious as spies and explorers. Therefore, they are continually preparing defenses and building fortifications, as those in China have done, because of their suspicions of these departures…"

About "the difficulty caused by thinking that China and other kingdoms can be converted, since it is not so", it pointed out:

"Likewise, one may reckon as a harm and a serious difficulty the settled opinion formed in Nueva España, Castilla, and Roma, through letters, that China or Cochin China, Camboja, Siam and other districts, will be converted. Therefore, it is necessary that His Majesty be undeceived and that people in Europe should be informed that, after all these departures, an embassy was sent by order of the governor, the bishop, and the community, who traversed all those kingdoms, even Malacca, yet now their contacts are more tightly close than ever; while the religious, who have gone without orders, have accomplished nothing more than to be insulted and maltreated, and to leave the pagans more haughty and more on their guard."

It concluded that "no secular person may leave the islands nor give the religious aid to leave them" and "that the religious come from España and Mexico for the islands and for no other place." [90]

The second attempt of Fr. Martin Ignacio de Loyola and the Augustinian friars

The Franciscan Spanish father Martin Ignacio Loyola, after his travels to Madrid, Rome and Portugal where he was given special powers and permits, in March 1585 went back to Goa with about 20 confreres and departed for Malacca in April 1586. In August 1856 he reached Macao, probably at the same time of the order of the viceroy of India, Duarte de Meneses, forbidding all the missionaries except the Jesuits to enter China

---

[90] Blair and Robertson, o.c., vol. 6. pp.194-197.

and Japan (April 12, 1586). On August 12, he proclaimed himself 'commissar of all the Franciscan friars in these parts of China'. He tried all the ways to enter China and towards the end of 1586 or early 1587, with Frs. Francisco Ramos and Francisco Nogueras, succeeded to reached Canton. There, although they proposed a Spanish embassy to Beijing with a 200 thousand *ducats* as present for the emperor, they received a bad welcome and were chased out, while their interpreter, a Chinese Christian from Macau, was flogged.

Meanwhile, in 1586, in order to facilitate their entrance into China, also the Augustinians, Francisco Manrique with Juan B. de Montoya, from the Philippines were sent to Macao. They arrived on November 1, and opened the convent of Our Lady of Grace (December 1586). The following year, they were joined by Frs. Diego de Espinar, (o Despinal), Nicolas de Tolentino and Luis Arias. Fr. Manrique, the rector of the Augustinian Convent, could visit Canton. On March 1, 1588, he gave the report of his trip to King Philip II. After the description of the city and the complaints about the prejudices of the Portuguese, he describes his talks with Fr. Ruggieri and Fr. Martin Ignacio. Fr. Ruggieri informed him about his trips inland (the first with one confrere, Antonio de Almeida, to Zhejiang and Jiangxi provinces, staying in Shaoxing, from November 1585 to July 1586, and the second to Guilin, Guangxi, from February to July 1587 [91]).

On July 6, 1587, Fr. Martin Ignacio with his confreres Fr. Francisco Ramos, Fr. Francisco Nogueras, and the Augustinians Frs. Francisco Manrique, Fr. Diego de Espinar, Nicolas de Tolentino, all back to Macao, wrote a letter to the king of Spain describing the difficulties of their work and the prejudices of the Portuguese and Jesuits against them.

In fact, Fr. Martin Ignacio had hard time: on August 6, 1586, the auditor Baltasar Arnão Lobo set up a trial against him, supported by the vicar gen-

---

[91] On November 25, 1588, Fr. Ruggieri was sent back to Europe by Fr. Valignao to arrange an embassy of the Holy See to China. On September 13, 1589 he arrived at Lisboa and in the following December to Madrid where he stayed five months, meeting the king. On June 14, 1590 he arrived at Naples, and on June 25 to Rome. Due to the death of four Popes one after the other, and the change of mind of the Jesuit superior, the Papal embassy to China was not pursued. Then, Fr. Ruggieri retired to Salerno, where he carried on intellectual and mapping work that make China better known in Europe. He died there on May 11, 1607.

eral Antonio Lopes da Fonseca, since he acted against the right of the Jesuits. The result was that Fr. Martin Ignacio had to leave Macau on July 10, 1587 for Manila, Mexico and Spain in order to report the events to the king.[92]

On February 18, 1595, King Philip allowed only Jesuits and Franciscans to reside in Macao, and repeated the 1589 prohibition for doing trade. Consequently, in the following year, the Augustinians had to cede their convent and leave. Diego de Espinar, Nicolas de Tolentino and Luis Arias met with drowning on their trip back to Manila in 1597.

After the attempt of Fr. Martin Ignacio, according to Fr. Jiacinto de Deus,[93] there was another one carried out by the Franciscan friars, Francisco Arruda and Francisco do Horto, who "went to Macao in the convent of Our Lady of Angels and very secretly entered to province of Canton, as the first door to the Empire of China: there, with the fervor of the divine love and zeal for the salvation of souls, they started to proclaim the necessity of the Christian faith for the salvation; but, they were not welcomed… and not allowed to go inland: so they returned to Macau and then to Malaca, sad for the lack of fruits and for the loss of many souls."

Attempts of the Spanish Dominicans

On September 17, 1581, the first bishop of Manila, the Dominican Domingo de Salazar, appointed by Gregory XIII on 6 February 1578, as bishop of Manila, suffragan see of Mexico (ordained bishop in Madrid in 1579), together with his confrere secretary Fr Christoval de Salvatierra, a group of Franciscans and Augustinian friars, as well as the first Jesuits, arrived in Manila from Mexico.

---

[92] Other sources say that he left on July 14, 1588, but it seems wrongly. He left Macau on the ship N. Senora de Buona Esperanza of Pedro Unamuno and reach Acapulco on 22 November. Later he went to Spain and up to 1594 he remained in the Convent of Cadahalso, St. Joseph's Province, and then he went to South America. In 1601 he renounced the bishopric of the Ascension (Paraguay) and was transferred to the Archbishoprich of Las Carchas. He died at Buenos Aires in 1612.

[93] Quoted by Manuel Texeira, *Os Franciscanos em Macau*, in Sepatata de 'Archivio Ibero-Americano', T. XXXVIII, 1978, Nos. 149-152, p. 340.

Pope Gregory XIII, in September and October 1582, issued two documents [94] allowing the foundation of the Dominican mission with the appointment of its vicar-general, "in the Philippine Island and in the kingdom of China". However, only in June 1586, 32 Spanish Dominicans were sent out for this destination, via Mexico. After many difficulties, only 15 of them led by Fr. Juan Castro arrived in Manila in 1587, while other three left Acapulco for Macao on the ship 'San Martin', three days earlier. On April 3, 1588, seven other fathers arrived in Manila, followed by Fr. Juan Crysostom of Aracena with several others in 1589, Fr Michael with 20 others in 1595 and, at least, as many in 1596 and 1598. The province of the Holy Rosary was established in 1592.

The three destined to China in 1586, Frs. Antonio de Arcediano (Marcedano), Ildefonso Delgado and Bartolomeu Lopez, met with a strong storm and their ship landed not in Macau but in the bay of Xiamen at Quanzhou on the coast of Fujian (April 1587). Here they were well treated, but soon sent to Macau. Bishop Domingo Salazar sent to the King of Spain, a report dated June 24, 1590, in which gives further details:

"What fully confirms me as to the truth of all this is the report which I received of the kind reception given in the province of Chincheo [Quannzhou] to a ship which the viceroy then governing Nueba España sent to Macan [Macao], and whose captain was Lope de Palacios, the brother of the auditor Palacios, auditor of Mexico. This ship was driven to Chincheo under stress of weather, and there everyone in her was well received, when the inhabitants of Chincheo learned that they were coming to trade in China. They persuaded them to go no farther, saying that they would give them a cargo there for their ship… The three Dominican religious who were in board the ship, were well received and lovingly treated by the mandarin of that province. He took them to the city and lodged them in his own house, giving them an apartment where they could celebrate mass. This they did with as much quiet and safety as if they had been at your court. The mandarin kept them with him for one week, after which he allowed them to go to their ship and proceed to Macan. I had this relation from the very religious who were there."[95]

Arriving at Macau on September 1, 1587, the three Dominicans were, first, guests of the St. Augustine's Convent. Then, they received in donation

---

[94] Blair &Robertson, o.c., vol 5, pp. 200-291.
[95] Blair & Robertson, o.c., vol. 7, pp. 212-238.

by the local vicar general Fr. Antonio Lopes da Fonseca, a house, which they took possession of on October 23, founding the convent of Our Lady of the Rosary. But only one year later, on June 10, 1588, the Provincial Council approved the new house, assigning as guardian Fr. Arcediano.

However, in 1589, the auditor Rui Machado was sent to Macau from India with the order to send away all the Spaniards. Therefore, before October 9, 1589, all the Spanish friars were substituted by Portuguese and left. Friar Arcediano and his companions went to Goa,[96] where he founded the famous convent of Santo Tomas. He started to teach theology and sent the other two to Spain and Rome to plead for the mission in China. But after six years of waiting, he lost hope and returned to Spain, where he continued teaching.

In Macao, meanwhile, the mestizo Portuguese-Chinese friar Antonio de S. Maria continued to take care of the convent. Other Portuguese Dominicans followed who changed the original church made of camphor wood and built the still extant Church of St. Dominic.[97]

In May 1590, there was another expedition from Manila to China of the Dominican Fathers, Juan de Castro and Miguel de Benavides, which is described by Bishop Domingo Salazar in a letter sent to the King of Spain, dated June 24, 1590.

"When the Portuguese expelled all the Castilian religious from Macan [Macau] and ordered them to go to India, and not to return here, two friars fled to the city of Canton, and thence they went to Chincheo by land, covering a distance of about one hundred leagues, without receiving any harm whatever; on the contrary, they were well treated, and the mandarin of Chincheo sent them back to this city in one of his own ships. The captain who brought them has visited me several times, and I have thanked him. At present these religious are in this city, and have spoken to me of what occurred to them on the journey from Macan to Chincheo, and of the presents, which the captain who brought them here from Chincheo gave them. From all the aforesaid we infer that what has been reported of the refusal of the Chinese kingdom, and of its rulers, to permit entrance to foreigners has been invention and

---

[96] According to another source, Fr. Lopez probably could remain in Macao for other three years.

[97] Manuel Texeira, *IV Centenario dos Dominicanos em Macau* (Fundação Macau, Impresa Oficial de Macau, June 1987)

slender by the Portuguese, who did this for their own private interests, fearing that their commerce with the Chinese would cease of the Castilians gained entrance there…"

Then, the bishop continues describing the life of the Chinese (or Sangleys) in Parian, near present Tondo and the evangelization work among them by the Dominicans, followed by the account of their decision to go to China.

"The Sangleys themselves told us to send fathers to their country to preach to them, saying that they would become converted without so much risk as here. After due consideration of the matter, the Dominican fathers and myself decided that it was necessary to go to China; for, if God permitted the religious to remain in that land, we could baptize the Sangleys here without cutting off their hair, or preventing them from returning to their country to rejoice in their children, wives and property. The Sangleys were much pleased in that decision; but there were differences of opinion regarding the manner in which the religious should go. The president thought that it would be best for them to go in a frigate accompanied by Spaniards; but the Chinese said that the friars should go alone, and not in the company of Spaniards…"

After two or three failed departures, with the assistance of two Chinese baptized, Francisco Zanco and Tomas Syguan, the departure of Frs. Juan de Castro, the Dominican provincial, and Miguel de Benavides was decided:

"So, Tuesday the 22nd of May of this year ninety, I went to the church of the Parian and said mass there; after which the two Sangleys who had offered their services went through a ceremony worthy of notice. They knelt before the altar where I said mass, and remained there for the space of two credos, speaking to one another in their own language and holding each other's hands; after that they embraced one another, and I learned afterwards that they had sworn to each other friendship and fidelity. From that place the fathers went to embark…"[98]

Both fathers returned to Manila in March 1591. Fr Miguel de Benavides soon sailed for Spain, where he worked as procurator of the province. Early in 1598, he returned to the Philippines as bishop of Nueva Segovia, but because of the death of archbishop Santibanez in Manila, he took his post. Archbishop Benavides in a letter to the King of Spain in the early 17th cen-

---

[98] Blair & Robertson, *The Philippine Islands*, vol. 7, pp. 212-238.

tury (he died on July 26, 1605) remarks that many of the Dominicans and Franciscans have been always motivated by the yearning for the missions of China and Japan.[99]

For the Chinese converts in Parian, a catechism in classical Chinese, *Catechismo Sino: Apologia de la Verdadera Religion* (Chinese catechism: Testimony of the true religion, Shilu prepared by of the Dominican Fr. Juan Cobo was published in 1593, eleven years before the famous Catechism of Fr. Ricci. Fr. Cobo also translated other books both in and from Chinese.

In 1593, another embassy left Manila, composed of Don Francisco de Castro and the Dominican Fathers Luis Gandullo and Juan de Castro. They headed for the city of Quanzhou, in Fujian, in search of the assassins of Governor Don Gomez Perez Dasmariñas, who had been killed in 25 October 1593 by some Chinese sailors off the coast of Batangas on his way to conquer Moluccas. But the embassy accomplished nothing.

Evaluation

From 1552 to 1583, there are registered, single or repeated, the attempts of 25 Jesuits, 17 of them priests and 8 scholastics, of 22 Franciscans, of whom 12 priests and 10 brothers or members of the third Order, of 2 Augustinians and of one Dominican.[100]

Another source [101] states:

"Thus, excluding the members of the Jesuit Residence in Macao, and counting each attempt of those who tried several times to enter China, there were thirty-two Jesuits (twenty-four priests and nine scholastics or lay-Brothers), twenty-four Franciscans (thirteen priests and eleven lay-Brothers or members of the Third Order), two Augustinians and one Dominican. If we count only the individuals and not the number of times, they tried to enter China, there were twenty-five Jesuits, seventeen of

---

[99] John SHUMACHER, *Readings in Philippines Church History* [Quezon City: Ateneo de Manila University, 1987], p.66.

[100] Pasquale D'Elia, *Fonti Ricciane* (Roma, La Libreria di Stato, 1942), vol. I, pp. 139-142.

[101] Joseph SEBES, "The Precursors of Ricci", in *Review of Culture* (Istituto Cultural de Macau, 1994).

them priests and eight scholastics or lay-Brothers; twenty-two Franciscans, of whom twelve were priests and ten lay-Brothers or members of the Third Order; two Augustinians; and one Dominican. This is by no means a complete listing. It is only a list of those who tried unsuccessfully, between 1552 and 1583, to penetrate China's self-imposed isolation and establish permanent Residence there."

Almost all the missionaries were arriving from Europe, the Portuguese and the Jesuits of other nationalities, through Lisboa, India and later from Macao, the Spaniard through the Philippines, via Fujian.

The role and the psychological attitudes of the individual personalities involved in these undertakings, both in the contacts with Chinese people and in the commitment to the evangelization of China, have not received due consideration.

As far as the contacts with Chinese authorities and people, the kindness and the mildness of one's personality, as in the case of Frs. Ruggieri and Ricci, contributed to smooth down the relationships. Stubbornness and prejudices from both sides created enormous obstacles. But the most important factor was the ability to speak Chinese, which allowed overcoming prejudices and misunderstandings, the increase in mutual esteem. Panela claimed that his influence and the friendship extended to him by Chinese were due to his mastery of Chinese language.

The external appearance and clothes as well as the behavior were also an important factor.

According to Pedro Sibal, who was in Macau when word had come from Guangdong that no more Spaniards were to go there from the Philippines, reported that he Chinese were not pleased at the Spaniards and at the Franciscans' visit, although his observation could be politically motivated:

"… and this witness knew that all those who went to China from this island [Luzon] would be killed by the coast-guards; and if any should get through, the guards who had missed them would be sentenced to death… This law has been put into effect since the Franciscan missionaries and others of these islands [the Philippines] had started to go to China. Previously they had not acted too rigorously, even though they had always maintained that no one should enter their country without official permission…"[102]

---

[102] Quoted in Gregory James (ed.), *Through Spanish Eyes*, o.c., p. xxxii.

As far as the commitment of the missionaries to the evangelization of China is concerned, it appears evident their spirit of strong persistence, caused mainly by the urgency of their missionary vocation: this was true especially for the Franciscans, who were heirs of a long tradition not only among the Mongols in China and in Asia, but also among the Muslims, started by the same St. Francis in Egypt in 1219. And even if the Spanish civil and religious authorities in Manila considered them insubordinate and foolish, they persisted in the attempts carried out not only without the due permit but also against the official order.

"The discalced Franciscan friars – complained Bishop Salazar to King Philip on June 18, 1583 [103] – *have borne much fruit among the natives of this land, and could do a great deal in the future if… they were not going to China or Vietnam. They have taken frigates to leave these islands four times, three in secret, without saying nothing either to the Governor or to me… I discussed this with the Commissioner and* Custos *of the Franciscans, and said that it was a very serious matter… to go in search of people we know little of, or among whom there was nothing to be gained… In spite of this, they decided to go there again…"*

Certainly, the firmness in this intent was not only due to the deep sense of the missionary vocation, but also to a certain spirit of adventure and curiosity, and to the attraction of the Chinese world, painted with wonderful colors (what later will be called 'the legend of China').

Such critiques, however, should not be limited only for the Franciscans: the Dominicans also carried out an attempt against the order of the Viceroy of India and of King Philip himself.

A positive appreciation for the Franciscans is that they always adopted humble and simple ways to enter China, and never thought about compromising with their civil government and being protected by its military force, as the Jesuits, the Augustinians and, for a time, even the Dominicans hoped for, as we will see in the next chapter.

---

[103] Quoted in Gregory James, *Through Spanish Eyes*, o.c., p. xxxii.

5

THE "MYTHS" ABOUT FR. MATTEO RICCI
(1552-1610)

First Myth: Fr. Ricci was the first to introduce China and Chinese culture to the West

Frequent is the statement that Fr. Ricci was the first person who disseminated Chinese culture in the West.

The first public writing of Fr. Ricci about China is dated 13 September 16: it was in Spanish and Ricci sent it to Juan Baptista Roman, who called it "a short report" and forwarded it to the king of Spain. But, before that date, we have seen several other authors who wrote about China and introduced Chinese texts in European languages, namely Juan Barros (1498-1570) who acquired Chinese books and maps, have them translated and sent to the Italian historian Paolo Giovio; Fr. Juan Cobo (1546/7-1593) who translated both into Chinese some works of Seneca and the *Doctrina Christiana* (Christian Doctrine), and from Chinese into Spanish in 1590 the *Mingxin Baojian* compiled by Fan Liben in 1393 under the title *Espejo rico del claro coràzon* (Precious Mirror of the Clear Heart); Fr. Martin de Rada, who we have seen wrote a Report on his travel and brought Chinese books from Fujian and have them translated; Fr. Alessandro Valignano who wrote an essay in Spanish on China in 1854, and others; Fr. Gaspar da Cruz, who, as we have seen, in 1556 published the firs book totally related to China with a great impact on Europe.

Second Myth: Ricci's translation of the Confucian Four Books

Common is the saying that Fr. Ricci has interpreted and translated into Latin the four Confucian Classic, namely, the Analects of Confucius, Mencius, Great Learning, and the Middle Way, which has become the basis for understanding China, "marking the beginning of sinology".

Ricci himself has few times mentioned that from 1591 to 1593 he has "paraphrased and annotated" in Latin the Four Books in order to help the young missionaries in their study of Chinese. Fr. Aleni, in his first biography of Ricci, stated that Ricci has sent a copy to Rome. However, this text has never been found. Francesco D'Arelli, in *Matteo Ricci e la traduzione Latina dei Quattro Libri* (1998) has specifically dealt with this "complicated and unsolved question."

The fact is that Fr. Michele Ruggieri also has started the translation of the Four Books in Latin. He himself brought his manuscript to Europe in 1588, and continued to correct the translation. A section of the *Daxue*, Great Learning, was published in the *Bibliotheca Selecta* of Possevino (pp. 581-584). The intervention of Fr. Valignano, who did not support Ruggieri for unclear reasons, with a letter to the Superior general Acquaviva, prevented the full publication. Fr. D'Elia in his collection of all the writings of Ricci,[104] about his "translation" of the Four Classics, states that it has "seemingly remained a manuscript" in the hands of the language students.

The first translation of the Confucian classic books, which attracted significant attention in Europe, was in *Confucius Sinarum philosophus* [Confucius, the Chinese philosopher], published in Paris in 1687.

Third Myth: Fr. Ricci as the Founder of the Catholic Mission in China

Michela Catto, writing about Ruggeri Pompilio (1543-1607, religious name Michele) states:[105]

"Although historiography and tradition attribute toe Matteo Ricci the title of the founder of the Mission in China, it was Ruggieri to set all the premises: pioneers in the language study, author of the first Christian work published in Chinese, the one who obtain the permit to establish a residence and the entry of other two companions. The building up of the myth of the mission of the Society of Jesus in Eastern Asia, also due to the Rites Controversy raised up almost immediately after the death of Ricci (1610), has induced to precociously develop a strict ling between the Jesuit China and Ricci and to reserve to Ruggieri a secondary role under many aspects, as the great quantitative difference of research and studies are dedicated to the two missionaries."

---

[104] D'Elia, *Fonti Ricciane*, o.c., II p. 33.
[105] Ruggeri Pompilio in *Dizionario Biografico degli Italiani* (vol. 89, 2017).

Chinese scholars, as Yu Liu, also emphasize the need to give greater attention to the role of Fr. Ruggieri.[106]

Fourth Myth: Frs. Alessandro Valignano and Matteo Ricci were the first to show concern for Chinese language and culture.

The method of "accommodation" or "adaptation", promoted by Frs. Valignano, Ricci and Ruggieri (although the latter is always neglected) included the mastery of the Chinese language, the openness to Chinese culture and values.

Their method, as we have seen, was first proposed by Fr. Melchior (Belchior) Nuñez Barreto. He was born in Porto, Portugal, in 1519 or in 1520 and joined the Jesuits at Coimbra around the year 1543. He was sent to India in 1551, where he could meet St. Francis Xavier and know about his plan to reach the Chinese Empire.

In May 1554, Fr. Melchior, then the Portuguese Provincial of the Jesuits, left Goa on his way to visit Japan, and spent the winter in Malacca. When in Malacca, on December 3, he was given an account written probably by Manuel de Chaves of the latter's experience of six years in a Chinese prison. [107]

The above quoted letters and proposals, sent to India by Fr. Barreto, concerning the ways for the evangelization of China, namely knowledge of the Chinese language and culture, embassy to the emperor, acquiring the favor of the higher authorities, are quite original and, certainly, were known by and have influenced the thinking of Fr. Alessandro Valignano (1539-1606), in deciding the so-called 'adaptation strategy' he would carry out through Frs. Michele Ruggieri and Matteo Ricci.

---

[106] In *Jesuits Missionaries in China and Tibet* (vol. 50, No. 4, May 2011).

[107] The text *Enformacão da China, que hum homen honrado que là esteue cativo seis annos, contou no collegio de Malaca ao Padre Mestre Belchior* (*Information on China, which an honorable man who was captive there for six years, related in the college of Malacca to Father Master Belchior*) was translated in Spanish as 'some letters of Jesuit fathers and brothers' in 1555 at Lisbon, and subsequently between 1556 and 1561 reprinted in several collections of Jesuit reports in various languages.

Fr. Barreto on June 5, 1556, continued his journey to Japan with two scholastics, leaving Bro. de Goes in Macau to learn the Chinese language. He reached Bongo, in Japan, in July 1556, where he stayed until November. His visit provided a strong encouragement to both missionaries and converts. Fr. Barreto reappeared in Macau on 4 December 1556 and found Bro. de Goes very ill. Therefore, he took him back to Goa. He reached Goa in February 1557 and in the following September made the solemn religious profession in the local College. Then, he was put in charge of the college in Cochin, and became vice provincial of India. He died in Goa on 6 October 1571.

Fifth Myth: Fr. Ricci was the one who first identified Cathay with China

The name of Cathay or Khitay was used to name Khitan (Qidan 907-1125) people and their empire in North China. Their language was related to the Mongolic language. The name was introduced to Europe via Islamic and Russian sources, and became "Cathay". Marco Polo who knew Mongol language spoke about Cathay, followed by the European travelers. In the modern era, the name Khitay is still used by Russian and Turkic peoples, to name China.

The Khitan people dominated much of Mongolia, Siberia and Northeast China by the 10th century, under the Chinese name of Liao Dynasty, and eventually collapsed by 1125. After the fall, many Khitans went westward to establish the Qara Khitay, in Central Asia, which lasted several decades before falling to the Mongol Empire in 1218. So, in the past before the Mongol conquest, Cathay differed from the Chinese Empire.

Jesuit fathers who entered China toward the end of 16th century realized that Chinese people called their own country Daming, Great Ming, from the ruling Ming Dynasty, while the name of China was only used by foreigners. In Europe the popular name was Cathay and, therefore, ignoring the history and the Mongolic origin of the name and the previous existence of a separate kingdom name Cathay, did not know whether Cathay was to be identified with China or not. They felt even puzzled. Jesuit missionaries in India were told by Muslims and Hindu sages that there was the country of Cataio or Cathay, which had many Christians; consequently, they were looking for it. However, from Ricci and their confreres in China were told

114

that this country, which they consider to be Cathay, did not have Christians. Ricci wanted to prove to them that the Cathay of Marco Polo was China and proposed to send somebody from India to China for this purpose. Ricci was concerned simply for a geographical purpose, showing however that he was ignoring both geography and history of Asia of his time. He also was not aware of information of previous authors about the then identity between Cathay ad China.

After the death of Gengis Khan, the Mongol Empire was divided in three Khanates, that had different historical development. Kublai Khan conquered Song Chinese Empire and established the Yuan/Mongol Dynasty. The Il-khanate in Persia was taken over by Muslim khans and split in other kingdoms, while in North-West China developed the Khanate of Oirat or Dzungeria, from the Eastern Mongol Empire. All the territories in North Asia under Mongol rule, including former states which had a consistent number of Christians and China, kept on being called by Turks and Russians, Cathay or Khitay, and European travelers adopted the name.

Later, the Mongols from China enlarged their control to other areas, including even Christian areas which however were undergoing the conversion to Islam. In 1368 the Mongol Dynasty in China was substituted by the Ming Dynasty. In Europe the whole area continued to be known as Cathay, without mush differentiation and several authors affirmed their identification.

In 1307, *The Flower of Histories of the East* first appeared in the city of Poitier, dictated in French by the Cilician Armenian statesman and general, Het'um (later monk of the Praemonstratensian Order), and then translated into Latin the same year by his secretary, Nicholas Falcon; it stated: *Qubilai-Khan ruled the Tartars for forty-two years. He converted to Christianity and built the city called Eons [Beijing] in the kingdom of Cathay, a city said to be greater than Rome. In this city Qubilai-Khan ruled as Emperor to the last day of his life.*[108]

Giovan Battista Ramusio (1485-1557) reported about the year 1550 what Haji Mohamet described him in Venice about places and life of "Cathay" identifying it with China, and about 1560 a 'Turkish dervish" ex-

---

[108] See website: Het'um the Historian's History of the Tartars.

plained to Auger Gislen de Busbeck customs and life in Cathay, he has visited, with characteristics typical of Chinese people. [109]

João de Barros in his *Terceira Decada da Asia*, published in Lisbon in 1563, freely exchanged the name of Cathay with China.

About the geographical identity between Cathay and China, it was Fr. Martin de Rada, who clearly informed European people that Cathay was China. He, back from the trip to China in 1575, wrote a *Relaçion Verdadera de las cosas del Reyno de Taibin* [Daming, Great Ming] *por otro nombre China y del viaje que el hizo el muy Reverendo padre fray Martin de Rada provinçial que fue de la orden del glorioso Doctor de la Yglesia San Agustin, quelo vio yanduvo en la provinçia de Hocquien* [Fujian] *año de 1575 hecha por el mesmo.* [110]

The first line of the text states clearly the identity between China and Cathay: "*News about the Great Taibin, that is about the kingdom that we call China, even if there is a certain confusion due to some old writings, such as that of the Venetian Marco Polo who calls it the Kingdom of Cathay.*

It is high time – wrote C.R. Boxer, in South China in the 16th Century – *that he* [Fr. Martin de Rada] *was given the credit which is due for being the first European writer on China who clearly and correctly identified this country with Marco Polo's Cathay."[111]*

Henry Yule in *Cathay and the Way Thither* wrote that the Italian geographer Giovanni Antonio Magini (1555-1617) was convinced of the identity of Cathay with China.[112]

Fr. Matteo Ricci seems to be unaware of the previous declarations: he affirmed his presumption about the identification of China with Cathay in a letter to the Superior general, Claudio Acquaviva, dated 13 October 1596, and confirmed it in his 18 October 1607 letter to the same Superior only after the declaration given by Bro. Bento de Goes (1562-1606), who went

---

[109] See Henry Yule, in *Cathay and the Way Thither*, vol. I, Notes XVII, XVIII and XIX (http://dsr.nii.ac.jp/toyobunko/III-2-F-b-2/V-1/page/0159.html.en).

[110] It was published by Juan Gonzalez de Mendoza, *Historia del gran Reyno de China* (Madrid, Pedro Madrigal Printer, 1586); see also Pablo Fernandez OP, *History of the Church in the Philippines, 1521-1898* (Metro Manila: Life Today Publications, 1988).

[111] C.R. Boxer, *South China in the Sixteenth century, o.c.,* pp. lxxv-lxxvi.

[112] Henry Yule, Cathay And The Way Thither Vol. 1 : Yule, Henry, Ed. : Free Download, Borrow, and Streaming : Internet Archive, vol I, p. cxliii.

from India to Gansu specifically for this purpose. He informed his confreres in India, who however did not fully believe because their concern was different and were still searching for the "Christian country", they were told about.

Sixth Enigma: The "Rules of Matteo Ricci"

In December 1706 the Kangxi Emperor, disgusted with the attitude of the Papal Legate, Charles Maillard de Tournon, required from the missionaries as a condition for remaining in China to follow "The Rules of Matteo Ricci" (利瑪竇的規矩 .) Surprisingly, these Rules of Ricci as Superior of the Jesuit China Mission have not come down to us. There is just a good summary of them, written in 1680 by the then Vice-Provincial of China, Giandomenico Gabiani, who, in his *Apologetic Dissertation on the Rites Permitted in the Chinese Church,*" produced just a list of documents on the subject supposed to go back to the time of Ricci. They comprise Ricci's instructions (*ordinationes*) issued in 1600 after consultation with his colleagues of the China Mission; further directives issued by Ricci in 1603 and confirmed by the Visitor Alessandro Valignano after consulting the whole Mission; some added 'resolutions' by Valignano; and a summary of these directives produced by Valignano "the same year" (presumably 1603). Gabiani sums these up as follows:

"All these early directives for this Church deal directly with inducing Christian morals and virtues in the Chinese neophytes, eradicating depraved and superstitious abuses; with tolerating prudently social rituals and civil cults according to the practice of the nation, and especially with rites for dead parents; grateful veneration of Master Confucius within the limits of common courtesy; with the licit use of Chinese sacred names as well as European; with covering the head as a sign of reverence with the Chinese; and finally with purifying the intention in fasting according to the Chinese custom...." [113]

---

[113] For more details see Paul A. Rule, "What were 'The Directives of Matteo Ricci' Regarding the Chinese Rites? In Pacific Rim Report, No. 54, May 2010 (http://www.ricci.usfca.edu/assets/prr54.pdf.).

The biography of Fr. Ricci, written by Fr. Giulio Aleni in 1630, states:[114]

"At the start of his last illness, the confreres warned him to leave his last will. Master Ricci answered: 'After my departure, open my bamboo wardrobe, you can find and read it.' At the opening of the wardrobe, indeed they found his last will, which disposed everything related to the church, and, well in order, all the letters of famous people, the ones received, the ones to send and the ones to keep."

However, all this documentation, including the dispositions of Ricci's last will, were not preserved. None of the letters received from and written to the Chinese literati, also got lost. We can read only Ricci's letters written to Jesuit superiors and friends.

In the collection of Fr. Ricci's remaining letters, one of the last ones was addressed to Fr. Francesco Pasio, the vice provincial of China and Japan dated 15 February 1609, a kind of last will. Ricci intended to answer to the two previous requests of Pasio, namely to get an official license from the emperor in order to assure the continuation of the presence of the Jesuits and to provide his hopes and expectations for the evangelization in China. About the first request, Ricci underlined the great difficulties in getting the license due to the bureaucratic procedure at the imperial court, and to the second he emphasized, first, to avoid the financial dependence from abroad and the political link with Macau, and then he proposed that "all the others should follow his style": namely, to give priority to the Confucian literati, and "engage war against all three sects, and even to fight some of the new opinions of the literati of this century [Neo-Confucians], who do not want to follow the ancient ones."

He speaks about his Style, not about his Rules: it consists in giving priority to Confucian mandarins and literati (he defended himself from the accusation of being "adulator of Confucians"), since he was convinced about the principles, then quite common, of *"cuius regio eius religio"* ("whose realm, his religion" that is, the religion of the rulers should dictate the religion of all people). But what kind of Confucian literati Ricci had in mind?

---

[114] Giulio Aleni, *La Vita di Matteo Ricci* (testo cinese con traduzione italiana, a cura di Gianni Criveller), Brescia, Fondazione Internazionale P. M. Ricci – Fondazione Civiltà Bresciana, 2010, p. 74.

He had in mind only Confucian mandarins and literati who followed the original teaching of the classical Confucian texts according to his interpretation and, at the same time, who attend the official rites just as a civic formality. He considered them "not believing in idols" or "atheist".

Fr. Ricci spoke about atheism in two places Nos. 170 and 199 of Fonti Ricciane:[115]

"The corrupt nature, if not helped by divine grace, degrades down by itself… among those who in these times avoid idolatry, very few are those who do not fall into atheism."

The second time, Ricci speaks of atheism when dealing with the tolerance toward religions: Chinese people

"turn out to remain without any religion, since they do not follow any in their heart. So, some openly confess their incredulity, others are cheated by the false persuasion of believing, and the majority of this people remains into the depth of atheism."

Atheism, in Ricci's mind and according to the comprehension of his times in Europe, was not understood as open opposition and negation of the existence of God, but just as the attitude of practical unbelief, of religious indifference, of utilitarianism of people using religion as a means for political, social, and moral life of the State. Ricci, with his mentality of clearcut boundaries of institutionalized religions (with a church, doctrine, rites and rule of conduct), did not accept the syncretistic religious attitude of Chinese people, but welcomed Confucians literati, even if they show a formal attitude in performing social and ritual ceremonies (to the ancestors and Confucius) just as external requirement, with the aim of converting them. He accepted the judgment of these Confucian literati that the rites were civil ceremony, since they were 'atheist' not believing in the idols. As they despised the ignorant populace, who was superstitious in performing those rites, Ricci also was not concerned about the conversion of the latter: they would spontaneously ask for baptism after the atheist "rulers" would be converted.

---

[115] O.c., vol. I, p. 110 and p. 132.

This was the Style of Ricci, which later seems to have been considered his Rules.

6

FR. ALONSO SANCHEZ AND THE "EMPRESA DE CHINA"

Submission of the Proposal

When the Spaniards began their conquest of the Philippines, they intended to use the archipelago as a base for contacts with other East Asian areas and for trade in spices. They were particularly concerned about China, of which they gained some knowledge from the Portuguese. China was a huge, rich and prosperous country, as well as a well-organized society with a highly refined culture. The Spanish royal court was interested in China not only because it was seen as the single nation outside Europe with the most advanced economy and culture, but also for the concern to bring such a highly civilized nation into the fold of Christianity. Moreover, China could turn out to be a source of prosperous trade, since its silks and ceramics were very popular.

As we have seen, it was the common mentality at that time in Europe as well as in the Philippines to justify theologically the Spanish conquest of the Philippines and of other neighboring lands. [116]

"Rumors of the wealth of the China trade at its source were not long in reaching the ears of the Spaniards. Andrès de Mirandola, the Royal Factor in the Philippines, wrote to Philip II from Cebu in 1569 that he had been told by Portuguese on that island 'how they traded and trafficked along the coast of China and Japan, and

---

[116] According to Eugenio Lo Sardo, the idea was not only common among the Spaniards in the Philippines, but also among the Portuguese: "A manuscript in the Madrid National Library entitled '*Sobre o modo che parece se deve ter non comeso de Conquista desta terra*', probably dating from the 1560s, makes plain the intention to attack southern China. The Portuguese felt that this plan could succeed if they employed 20 or 30 galleons and some 100 Indian small vessels. They intended to use about four or five thousand soldiers. This Portuguese plan was based upon other military campaigns already carried out in the Orient..." (E. Lo Sardo. "Valignano and the Conquest of China", in *Acts du VII Colloque Internationale de Sinologie*, Chantilly 1992, (Taipei –Paris, Ricci Institute, 1995), p. 294.

how this was the commerce which supported them, for it is the greatest and most profitable trade which has been seen hitherto'. The reports of the Portuguese were partly confirmed by two stray Chinese traders whom Mirandola interrogated; but they assured him that the Emperor of China did not allow the Portuguese to settle ashore because he was nervous about a potential foreign aggression. Like a true conquistador, Mirandola concluded his letter by forecasting that the conquest of China would prove an easy matter for the Spaniards if the King would sanction this enterprise in due time."[117]

Another suggestion for this kind of enterprise comes from a letter of Fr. Martin de Rada to the Marquis de Falces, viceroy of Nueva España (Mexico), from Cebu, July 8, 1569, which contains the Rada's first recorded reference to China:

"If His Majesty wishes to get hold of China, which we know to be a land that is very large and rich and of high civilization, with cities, forts, and walls much greater than those of Europe, he must first have a settlement in these islands: first, because we cannot pass safely among the so many islands and shoals that lie along the coast of China with ships of high freeboard, but must use oared vessels; secondly, also, because in order to conquer a country so large and that has so vast a population, one must have aid and refuge near at hand, for any contingency that might arise. However, as I have been informed both by Portuguese and by Indians who trade with the Chinese, as well as by a Chinese who was captured a while ago in a junk, the people of China are at all warlike. They rely entirely on numbers and on the fortification of their walls. It would decapitate them, if any of their forts were taken. Consequently, I believe (God helping), that they can be subdued easily and with few forces..."[118]

A further proposal related to the conquest and conversion of China came from Dr. Francisco de Sande and Diego Garcia de Palacios (Manila, 2 June 1576).

"Possibly one reason for Sande's cavalier attitude towards the Chinese, was his conviction that they could easily be conquered by a Spanish expeditionary force from Manila with the assistance of Japanese and Filipino auxiliaries, 'who are much

---

[117] C.R. Boxer, *South China…*, o.c., pp. xl-xli.
[118] Reported in Blair & Robertson, *The Philippine Islands, o.c.*, vol. 34, pp. 227.

braver than they are'. The bellicose governor begged his royal master seriously to consider the prospect of the conquest of China, for it is very right that such a just and great king's hands and laws should encircle the globe'. This crazy project received plenty of support from clerical and military hotheads at Manila; but, unlike the men on the spot, the Crown councilors at Madrid clearly saw the monstrous folly of such an undertaking. Their opinion was echoed by King Philip II who sharply rebuked his headstrong governor, 'As regards the conquest of China which you think should be undertaken forthwith, it has seemed to us here that this matter should be dropped; and that, on the contrary, good friendship should be sought with the Chinese. You should not act or collaborate with the piratical enemies of the said Chinese, nor give them any excuse to have just cause of complaint against our people'."[119]

The role of Fr. Alonso Sanchez and the Involvement of the Italian Jesuits

Spain had sent a number of diplomatic missions to China in order to gain a trading port on its coast, but without achieving its objective. These frustrations created a climate favorable to push for a military conquest of China.

On 14 March, 1582, as we have seen, the Jesuit Fr. Alonso Sanchez, who had arrived in Manila in 1581, was sent as ambassador by the governor Gonzalo Ronquillo to solicit the acceptance of Philip II as king of both Spain and Portugal from the people in Macao, and to obtain a trading port from China.

Fr Alonso Sanchez met Ruggieri in Canton and was helped by the latter to get the permit to reach Macao, where he went in May 1582. There he met again Ruggieri, certainly in November at his return from the misadventure in Formosa, but probably even during the month of June, after Ruggieri returned from Zhaoqing and Canton. They certainly discussed about the mission in China.

In the previous March, Fr. Alessandro Valignano had arrived to Macau from Japan, with the four Japanese princes in their journey to Europe. On

---

[119] C.R. Boxer, *South China…*, o.c., Introduction, p. l. The statement is based upon the *Proposal of Dr. Francisco de Sande and Diego Garcia de Palacios to attempt the conquest and conversion of China*, Manila, June 2, 1576 and the letter of King Philip to F. de Sande, April 29, 1577.

August 7, Frs. Pasio and Ricci also arrived in Macau from India, and in November they too could meet Fr. Sanchez. During his months in Macao, Sanchez discussed with all of them about the best strategy for China. He, who was certainly a strong-willed man, did not hesitate to express in various letters, some to Claudio Acquaviva the Superior General himself, his firm criticism of Valignano's accommodation approach and the way he was running the local Jesuits establishment. Valignano, who left Macao on December 31, 1582, reacted strongly to this criticism from Goa.

Few days earlier on the 17th of the same December, Frs. Ruggieri and Pasio also have left Macao for Zhaoqing, while Sanchez and Ricci stayed in Macao until the departure of the former for Manila. Ruggieri and Pasio from Zhaoqing exchange correspondence with Sanchez in Macao.

On February 13, 1583, Sanchez and some other missionaries, among whom his own group and the Franciscan Jeronimo de Burgos with his companions, left Macao and reached Manila on March 27. Here he started to propose *la Empresa de China*. This suggestion found a strong support with the acting governor Diego Ronquillo, the royal 'factor' Juan Baptista Roman and other local clergy.

In 1583, from April to June, Fr. Sanchez reported to Bishop Salazar 'decisive documentation on the failure of the evangelization' in China and consequently the right of the king of Spain to conquer the empire, stating that he reached that opinion after consulting 'a dozen of authoritative people'. Bishop Salazar was convinced of the goodness of the proposed *Empresa*. He gathered information from other witnesses, during two months, namely, on April 19, from the Portuguese soldier, Pedro Sibal (50, who traveled to China for 27 years and remained in Chinese prison for four years), from Sebastián Jorge Moxar (38, a Portuguese captain who sailed regularly to China for 19 years) and Gaspar Fernández de Medeyros (46, a Portuguese soldier with family in Macao for 25 years); on April 26, from the Portuguese soldier Cristoval Cardoso (25, who have been sailing to Macau and China for five years); on May 2, from the Castilian military officer Francisco Dueñas (40, who accompanied the Franciscans in 1579); on May 12, from Juan de Feria (45, who was a participant of the missionary expedition led the Franciscan Jerónimo Burgos in 1582); and at last, on June 13 and 14, the participants to the embassy to Macao of Fr. Alonso Sánchez, the ship pilot Alonso Gómez (aged 28) and the Spanish sailor Juan Baptista Barragán (aged 27).

On April 19, 1583, Bishop Salazar wrote to King Philip II and Pope Gregory XIII about it (*Información sobre los impedimentos a la predicación en China realizado por el obispo Domingo de Salazar para el Papa Gregorio XIII y el Rey Felipe II. Manila 19 de Abril de 1583*), emphasizing the obstacles created by the Chinese authorities against the preaching of the Gospel in China and, on the following June 8, he again wrote to the king underlining the many reasons that could justify the military enterprise.

"The hindrance put by the rulers of China to the preaching of the Gospel is the most legitimate title Your Majesty has to enter with armed hand into that kingdom…"

In March 1583, Ruggieri and Pasio had to leave Zhaoqing and returned to Macau. In the following summer, Frs. Ruggieri and Ricci, since Pasio had left for Japan, tried to go back to China and in early September, at last, succeeded to return to Canton and settle in Zhaoqing.

Towards the end of 1583 and in the early months of 1584 from Zhaoqing Frs. Ruggieri and Ricci wrote letters to the Spanish Governor and the Bishop of Manila, updating them on the good development of China Mission, and asking for financial support. Fr. Sanchez also received letters from Ruggieri and Ricci. There in Manila the proposal to send a Spanish embassy to China became popular. In the correspondence, the proposal of the embassy in order to hand the presents of the King of Spain left in Mexico could be forwarded to the Chinese Emperor, was also raised.

All these events strengthened the idea of the *Empresa* in everybody, most probably under the push of Fr. Sanchez, who convinced the acting governor Ronquillo to send him back to Macao with the 'real factor' Juan Baptista Roman, under the pretext of searching for the galleon St. Juan, whose crew has carried out a mutiny. They could also solicit a "Spanish embassy" to China through the help of the Jesuits Fathers Ruggieri and Ricci in Zhaoqing, to whom they were bringing subsidies and gifts from the Governor and the Bishop.

In fact, at the beginning of May 1584, Fr. Sanchez returned to Macau with Roman. From Macao he had an exchange of correspondence with the Italian Jesuits in Zhaoqing asking them to arrange a visit of Sanchez and Roman to the Viceroy in Zhaoqing in order to promote the plan of the Spanish Embassy. Ruggieri and Ricci answered them, providing information on China, but underlining the difficulty rising from the impossibility for the Chinese Emperor to estimate the greatness of Spain, and, through them, they sent letters to the viceroy of Mexico. Sanchez and Roman could not go to Zhaoqing, as desired.

On July 5, Fr. Sanchez wrote a letter to the Vice-provincial of Japan, Fr, Gaspar Coelho, stating that it is impossible to convert China just through preaching without war: Frs. Ruggieri and Ricci, according to him, have written that we have to find a way to keep peace with the viceroys and the emperor of China, but he considered it fruitless, and so there was the need to "plan the war in order to assure the peace of the evangelizers" (*ad evangelantium pacem*).[120]

In September, Roman and Sanchez met Ruggieri who went down to Macao to hand the report about China and its resources, written by Fr. Ricci, for Roman, who sent it to King Philip II in a dispatch dated on September 8.[121]

On October 1, Sanchez and Roman left Macao. After their return to Manila on June 6, 1585, Fr. Sanchez continued to support the plan of the *Empresa de China*, until 1586, when the *Audiencia* in Manila took the formal decision to propose it to the Council of Indies and to the King Philip II, sending the Jesuit to Spain to explain and plead for it.

The Interpretation of the Event by Fr. Ricci

Fr. Ricci, in his History,[122] describes the whole event in the following terms:

---

[120] Tacchi Venturi, *Opere storiche del P. Ricci*, t. II, pp. 425-427.

[121] D'Elia, *Fonte Ricciane*, o.c., vol. I, p. 215 note 1: "About the whole affair of the Castille embassy, remain two letters of Roman to King Philip II, written from Macau on June 25 and 27, 1584, and other two letters of Sanchez, written to the same King, from Macau, dated June 22 and 27. According to these letters, both Roman and Sanchez, toward the end of June, still were hoping to be able to reach Zhaoqing and Beijing to deal with the affair of the sending of the presents of the King of Spain. The same letters inform that Ruggieri and Ricci sent also to the Viceroy of New Spain, that is Mexico, a letter to forward to King Philip."

There is also this dispatch dated September 8, although the report of Ricci brings the date of September 13.

[122] D'Elia, *Fonti Ricciane*, o.c., vol. I, ch. VI, nos. 269-272.

"269. *The Governor of the Philippines, with his counselors and the Bishop of Manila decided to contribute some help also from their part* [to the China Mission]; *and at the same time, through the intervention of the Fathers* [in China] *to gain some place in Guandong province, where their ships could trade and get some profit for their country. And for this purpose, they sent to this land a father of the Society, named Alfonso Sanci* [Alonso Sanchez] *and the Factor (Exactor) of the King of Spain, by name Giovanni Battista Romano* [Juan Batista Roman], *who was a very serious and prudent person, through whom they wrote to the Rector in Macau and to the Fathers of Sciaochino* [Zhaoqing], *sending together a good gift of silver and other things, among which a spring clock, very sophisticated.*

The summary of all the content of the letters was that they very much rejoiced of good results given by God for the entry of the Society [of Jesus] *in that great kingdom, so much desired by the King and the whole Christendom, and that they, also moved by the obligation of all the faithful to help such an enterprise, wanted to inform them that years before the King of Spain had sent a magnificent present to be handed to the King of China, present that was in Mexico of New Spain. Because of this, they asked the Fathers to procure from the Viceroy of Guangdong the license to send an embassy of Spain with this present to the King of China. On such an occasion, the Fathers could go to the Court, have audience with the King and obtain the permit to spread the Gospel in the whole kingdom, and in order to favor all this, they were sending some silver for the expenses and that clock; and that the Exactor, on behalf of the King, should provide everything necessary for the expenses. Consequently, Fr. Alfonso and the Exactor Juan Batista insisted to get the permit for themselves to go to Zhaoqing to discuss the affairs directly with the Viceroy.*

270: Fr. Francisco Capral, who was the Rector in Macau, wrote to the Fathers inviting them to deal the affair with the Viceroy in such a way that no harm should be caused to the enterprise of China. Therefore, the Fathers started to deal with it with prudence, through an employee of the palace of the Viceroy, without making use of the name of the Fathers, nor of anybody else of their house.

He first went with the Memorial prepared for the Viceroy to show it to the new Lincitao (Superintendent of the Western Regions), in order to see his reaction and opinion. He was so pleased with the news and approved so willingly the affair that he himself ordered to be taken on the sedan chair to the place of the official in charge of receiving and presenting memorials to the Viceroy, approving the ones he himself likes, and advised him to immediately submit that memorial to the Viceroy, since it was something very profitable and honorable for them, and this he did.

And the Viceroy also approved it and sent it back, according to the custom of his court, to the Haidao (the sea high officer) of Guangdong, so that he could register that proposal and relate the truth of the matter after due investigation: it was a sure signal that he wanted the coming of the ambassadors with their presents."

No. 271 points out the contrary intervention of the Macau Portuguese who were afraid that the Spaniards were planning to start trade with China; therefore, they opposed the dealing for a Spanish embassy. The monopoly of contacts and trade with China should be kept by Portugal. They wrote to the Fathers warning them not to get involved in the affair and pushed Fr. Capral to write them on the same line:

"With these things, very different from what they were thinking, the Fathers remain quite perplexed not knowing whether to give up the affair or how to continue it. At last, they found out that the best was to refrain from doing anything new.
272: The Haidao waited in vain for the appearance of the signer of the Memorial, who was the interpreter of the Fathers. He sent a message to the Zhixian (sub-prefect) of Heung Shan (香山 Xiangshan) asking him to get information whether any ambassador had arrived in Macao with presents for the Emperor of China or not. The latter was informed by the Exactor and other Spaniards in a positive way, verifying all the details of the memorial in a favorable way, due to the large present they gave to those who went to collect information.
But, on the other hand, the Macao citizens gave a very different information, saying that they were people of another kingdom, different from Portugal, who should not be allowed to enter, since it will create lots of divisions and conflicts among the people of the two kingdoms.
The Haidao, after all this information, issued an edict, hung on the doors of Guangzhou, relating all the details of the affair, complaining about the interpreter who did not appear at the audience. And it concluded stating that, if that kingdom which wanted to come to give presents to the Emperor is the same as that of the foreigners in Macau, there is no need to come since no license should be issued; but if it is another one, who have already come several times, it could come. At the end, he ordered the official of Xiangshan to forbid such men to submit to the Viceroy similar memorials and to punish them severely."

Ricci's conclusion was: *And God wanted that this affair ended without giving any harm to the house and residence in Zhaoqing.*

The motivations that pushed Ruggieri, Pasio and Ricci to turn to the Spaniards in Manila for help and support were, according to Eugenio Lo Sardo, the following:

"The treaties which followed the unification [between Spain and Portugal] had established Portugal's commercial independence from Spain, and the Portuguese Padroado remained a separate administrative entity to be distinguished from the

Spanish Patronato Real. So, from the legal point of view the monopoly of the traffic in and out of China and Japan remained firmly in the hands of the Macao traders… They also lost no opportunity of painting a totally negative picture of their Hispanic brethren to Chinese mandarins. In those years of dire political instability, Valignano left, in 1582, East Asia for Goa, in the train of Japanese princes journeying to Rome. His long absence – which was originally intended to have been even longer since it was suggested he should return to Italy – left the tiny mission in Zhaoqing without his crucial guidance and vital financial support, right in its most delicate initial moment. Ruggieri did not enjoy a particularly warm relationship with the Portuguese in Macao and the Jesuit Superior resident there. He was thus forced to ask for money and support from the Jesuits in the Philippines, particularly from Sanchez whom he had met and helped in 1582 on a diplomatic mission. Sanchez and the Governor of Manila, Gonçalvo Ronquillo, responded enthusiastically to Ruggieri's plea for aid… "[123]

Sanchez was indeed full in favor of the idea of a military enterprise which would enable the Spaniards to set up commercial dealings with southern China and force the Chinese to be more tolerant of the missionaries. Sanchez was anxious to obtain more information about China, especially details about her geography, her administrative structure and her armed forces. Ricci drew up a long and detailed report for them. Ruggieri could offer verbal advices on various matters.

The Decision of the Audiencia (1586)

The Manila *Audencia* (Assembly) of 19 April 1586 decided to hold a general assembly on the following day, to which all the high authorities, both civil and religious, were invited as representatives of the then 140 Spanish settlers.

The proposal to "enter China" was accepted and decided by all the members of the *Audencia*, together with the text of the Memorial. [124] Here the introduction letter by the secretary:

---

[123] E. Lo Sardo. "Valignano and the Conquest of China", a. c., pp. 295-300.

[124] See full text of the following documents in http://www.fullbooks.com/The-Philippine-Islands-1493-1898.html (part 3).

"In the city of Manila, on June 26 of the year 1586, the following persons met in the royal building: The honorable president and auditors of the royal Audiencia of these islands, and his Majesty's fiscal of the Audiencia; Don Fray Domingo de Salazar, bishop of the Filipinas; and the religious, the captains, the magistrates, and the municipal officers of this city—who hereunder signed their names. They met to discuss fully the matters contained in this document, about which Father Alonso Sanchez as procurator-general of this country, and acting in its name, is to confer with his Majesty, and solicit aid from him, that the prosperity and colonization of these islands may continue to increase, and that God and his Majesty may be served. The above articles having been read, as they are here recorded, de verbo ad verbum, *all the above persons declared, unanimously and with one consent and opinion, that this memorial was properly drawn up; and that Father Alonso Sanchez should communicate all its contents to his Majesty, and other matters as seemed to him necessary. The above honorable persons made the required attestations to the document, and signed it with their names, as did other persons. I, the clerk of the court, attest this.*

(signed by Alonso Beltran, the Secretary, followed by other thirty signatures)

The text on the "Proposed Entry into China", in the tenth chapter of the Memorial, which was drafted by Fr. Sanchez in the Bishop's residence, reads:

"The person who is sent as an eye-witness will give his Majesty a brief relation of the vastness of China, of the abundance of its fruits and provisions, of the richness of its merchandise, and the great quantity of gold and silver, quicksilver, copper, iron, and other metals; of the immensity and certainty of the treasures, and the infinite amount and variety of the products of the handicrafts and of human industry; and, above all, the endless things that may be said about the people and their life,

---

"On the back of the Sevilla copy are written…: "1: There was an assembly of all the estates, who resolved to send a person to his Majesty; and all appointed Father Alonso Sanchez: April 19, in the year 86. 2: On the fifth of May, 86, the royal Audiencia of Manila appointed Father Alonso Sanchez as envoy. 3: On the twentieth of June, 86, the bishop and cathedral of the city of Manila appointed the same. 4: On the sixteenth of April, 86, the bishop and the superiors of the religious appointed the same. 5: On the 25th of June, 86, the judiciary, magistracy, and *cabildo* of Manila appointed the same. 6: On the twenty-eighth of May, the master-of-camp and the captains of the Filipinas Islands appointed the same."

*health, peace, and plenty; and how, with and by all this, there is offered to his
Majesty the greatest occasion and the grandest beginning that ever in the world was
offered to a monarch. Here lies before him all that the human mind can desire or
comprehend of riches and eternal fame, and likewise all that a Christian heart, desirous of the honor of God and his faith, can wish for, in the salvation and restora-
tion of myriad souls, created for Him, and redeemed by His blood, and now deluded
and possessed by the devil, and by his blindness and wickedness…"*

About "the right and ground for this entry", the Memorial leaves to Fr.
Sanchez the duty of the explanation:

*"As for the right and justification which we have for entering and subduing this land,
the father who is going to España will discuss and explain this to his Majesty, as he
has considered it long and often with the Castilians here, as well as elsewhere…"*

The forces, equipment and supplies necessary are enumerated in detail,
and also what part of these can be furnished by the Philippines themselves:
it will be sufficient for ten or twelve thousand men to come from España,
either Spaniards, Italians, or other subjects of Spain; the governor of these
islands should also be the commander of the expedition; India should provide 500 hundred slaves; troops could be recruited also from Japan, with
the help of the Jesuit fathers. The fleet which is expected to come from
Spain with men and supplies should land in Cagayan, Luzon; the routes
which may be taken by those vessels are described, and that by the Strait of
Magellan is recommended as the shortest and safest.

About the role and the help from the Portuguese:

*"It is important that his Majesty give the Portuguese a part in this conquest, because
they could greatly aid by the experience that they have of the seas, lands, and people
of these regions. Their army should not come together with the Castilians, nor should
the assault be made from one side alone; but they should go by Canton, and the
Castilians should go by way of Chincheo* [Quanzhou, bay of Xiamen, Fujian], *as
nearly as possible at the same time…*
*His Majesty should procure and bring about that the general of the Society of Jesus
should command and ordain to the fathers in Japan, not to hinder the bringing of
this reinforcement of Japanese, and whatever may be needed therefore; and to this
end he should send a father sufficiently commissioned, who should be an Italian*
[probably Fr. Pasio].
At the proper time and juncture, which will be before the news of the expedition

has come to the knowledge of the Chinese, the fathers of the Society who are within the borders of China, in the city of Joaquin [Zhaoqing, Frs. Ruggieri and Ricci], should be withdrawn, that they may give information to the armies about what they know of the country, its strength, and its military forces and supplies; and whatever other dangers or reasons for caution they have in mind. They will also serve as interpreters, and persuade the Chinese to allow the Spaniards to enter in peace, and to hear and receive the preachers, and accept the religion sent them by God. They will tell the Chinese of the protection which his Majesty desires to offer them, so that they may receive the Spaniards without fear; and how great a favor he is doing them in freeing them from the tyrannies of their mandarins, and relieving them from the yoke of slavery that they at present bear, leaving them in freedom of body and soul, and exacting nothing but an acknowledgment for this gracious act. To this end the fathers should receive many chapas [pass], and scatter over the whole of China, and be of use in any other way that their life in the country may make possible. These should be the instructions of the general of the Society of Jesus to his commissioner."

The recommendations emphasize the religious purpose:

"Let it be known and understood that what has heretofore been said and decreed respecting preparations for war is not meant to convey the impression that we should or could act as if we were dealing with Turks, Moors, and other races who are unfriendly, and the declared enemies of our belief and our king. For these people neither know nor understand it, and are not ill-inclined. The forces are to be sent merely to escort and protect the preachers of the faith and subjects of the king who sends them, and to see that they are allowed to enter the land, and may preach where they choose and consider it needful, and so that those who hold the government shall not hinder the others from hearing and receiving the doctrine. They will see to it also that conversion shall go on without intimidation, and without danger that through threats of punishment any of those already converted should relapse or apostatize."

The gains which would result from the conquest of China are enumerated, giving priority to the religious one:

"The first of the many and enormous benefits of this conquest, if it be rightly ordered and carried out, is that the knowledge of God and of Jesus Christ His Son, our Lord — which has commenced in these lands so remote and distant from the church and the support of the Catholic kings. The second: No one, if he has not seen it, can imagine or comprehend the infinite multitude of souls that will thus come to the knowledge and adoration of their Creator...

It will be necessary to establish immediately a large number of schools, where our writing, language, and literature may be easily and quickly learned...

From the beginning a large number of churches and monasteries will be founded, not only for the purpose above mentioned, but especially to instruct in our faith, doctrine, and mode of life.

There will be no difficulty in pacifying and converting the peasants, countrymen, and villagers, who are so numerous that nearly all the land is covered with villages; for they are quite simple and unsophisticated, and suffer great oppression and tyranny. With the women, who are very numerous, there will be even less difficulty in introducing the faith, because of their virtue and great reserve, which is remarked by all who know of them — to such a degree that they lack only Christianity to be much beyond us in all matters of morality.

It will result in time in preventing the entry of the cursed doctrine of Mahoma [Mohammad], *which has already infected almost all the other realms, and its establishment there..."*

Dealing with "other special advantages", the economic benefits are mentioned:

"Those vessels, or as many others, can be loaded every year with gold, raw silk, and all sorts of silken fabrics—taffetas, satins, damasks, etc.; with musk, chests inlaid with ivory, boxes, wrought and gilded curtains, and whatever kinds of furniture, appliances, ornaments, and jewels are used by man; and many a web of linen cloth, of every sort and kind. Thus, there would be no necessity for bringing to España, as is now done, these goods from foreign lands; and our money and wealth would be retained in España..."

Other advantages derive from "the amount of the rents and taxes", which can be levied; many estates can be divided and distributed among our people; a great part of the Spanish people could go and settle there.

"On account of the great virtue, modesty, submissiveness, and beauty of the Chinese women, they would have proved to be excellent wives for the Spaniards; thus, the two peoples would mingle, and all would be united, fraternal and Christian."

Minor advantages, that will arise from the conquest of China, are also listed: the establishment of numerous episcopal sees; the foundation of new military orders, and the extension of the old ones; the creation of many titled lords, and appointments of viceroys for the conquered provinces.

China, thus subdued, will be a vantage-ground from which Spain can control all Asia and a land-route to Europe. Chinese colonists can be imported into the Philippines, "and thus enrich themselves and this land." And finally, "the immediate occupation of China still forestalls any advance into the Far East by the French, or the English, or any other heretical nation." [125]

The Commitment and Difficulties of Fr. Sanchez

Fr. Sanchez left Manila and set sail for Mexico at the end of June 1586 on the galleon San Martin, arriving at Acapulco in January 1587 after a stormy six-month trip. There he found people who did not agree about the *Empresa de China,* and tried to detain him. They asked the opinion of Fr. José de Acosta who was passing through Mexico City in his way back from Peru to Spain, who opposed the proposal of war. But Fr. Sanchez convinced of the importance of his mission, wrote two memoranda, one for the Spanish government on 15 March 1587 and a second for the Superior general, Fr. Claudio Acquaviva, on 22 March 1587, who did not agree with his opinion. Fr. Acosta, on his part, back to Spain in 1587, wrote the *Historia natural y moral de las Indias,* about his observations of America, and in the following year, another, controversial book, *De promulgatione Evangelii apud Barbaros, sive De Procuranda Indorum salute,* in which he strongly criticized the treatment given to the Indians by the Spanish officials. His primary objections were the conditions that the missionaries condoned. Acosta wrote, "not only have we failed to bring them the news of Christ with sincerity and honest faith, but we have betrayed in our deeds what we professed in our words."

Acosta's position, however, was not totally against the plan, since he proposed a middle course: he conceded on the one hand that the unbelievers

---

[125] The main signatures are: the Governor Dr. Santiago de Vera, the Bishop of the Filipinas, the licentiate Melchor Davalos, the licentiate Pedro de Rojas, the licentiate Ayala, the Archdeacon of Manila, Antonio Sedeno, rector, Alonso Sanchez, Fray Diego Alvarez, provincial, Hernan Suarez, Fray Juan de Plasencia, custodian of the order of St. Francis, Fray Vicente Valero, guardian, Fray Alonso de Castro Raymundo, Fray Pedro de Memdieta, Fray Juan de Quinones, canon Don Juan de Armendariz, canon Luis de Barruelo, etc., and last, Alonso Beltran, the Secretary.

must never be coerced into conversion, but on the other hand, he held that a purely apostolic procedure was impossible under the existing circumstances; consequently, the missionaries were to follow the apostolic methods so far as possible, but, whenever necessary, they should have the protection of the civil power.

On May 18, 1587, Sanchez departed for Seville, Spain, arriving in September. From there he proceeded to Santarem in order to present before the King and the Royal Council the important proposal. On December 15, he had the first meeting with Philip II leaving him all the documents and the Memorial, as well as his own memorandum. The king was then worried about the invasion of England, preparing and sending the great *Armada* in January 1588 (and soon lost it). But in March he appointed a commission to study the Memorial and the documents, which worked from March to July, together with Sanchez. Philip II examined the Memorial and the documents personally in July or August. Fr. Sanchez, in his memorandum, has fully justified the Spanish rule of the Philippines. The solution of the problem of abuses, injustices and wrongdoings of the officials should be solved by choosing the best man to represent the Crown. He suggested Gomez Perez Dasmariñas as the new Governor for the Philippines. King Philip accepted this suggestion, but without pressing his advocacy for the dubious *Empresa de China*.

"When Sanchez was still in Madrid expediting the affairs of the Philippine colonists (1587-88), there happened to be there at the same time two religious who were trying to get Philip II to approve and finance a project of theirs for the conversion of China. They were Fray Juan Volante, a Dominican, and Fray Geronimo de Burgos, the Franciscan whom the Macao authorities sent back to Manila with Sanchez in 1583. Their project was to transport two large missionary expeditions - 60 Dominicans and 100 Franciscans - from Spain to China via the Philippines at the king's expense. In order that the authorities at Manila might place no obstacle on their way, they asked that these missionaries be exempted while in transit from any subordinate civil or ecclesiastical jurisdiction. Once on Chinese soil, they were to be given complete freedom of action, for their plan was to enter the Chinese Empire without armed escort or civil protection of any kind. Nevertheless, Volante and Burgos had had no success in arousing official interest in it, although they preceded Sanchez at court by almost three years (1584-85). Finally, sometime after Sanchez arrival, they were given a hearing by the Council of the Indies, but getting some trouble in it. It was probably at this juncture that they appealed to Sanchez for assistance but he refused. He explained his reasons in a letter to Volante dated 27 July 1588. He was, he said, the agent at court of the Philippine colonial assembly, and

one of the petitions which he had to submit in his behalf was that no Spanish missionaries be permitted, at least for the time being, to go to China. The repeated attempts of missionaries from the Philippines to enter China had all ended in failure and had merely served to arouse the hostility of the Chinese authorities against the Spaniards, whom they suspected of spying out their country with a view of a subsequent invasion. They also placed the Portuguese, whose foot-hold at Macao was at best precarious, in a most embarrassing position; the authorities at Macao were quite insistent that the Spaniards desist from any more such attempts; and since the Portuguese were now equally Philip's subjects, their interests had to be taken into consideration. Hence, Sanchez said, he would be acting contrary to his mandate if he assisted Volante in his project instead of trying to dissuade him from it and doing his best to obtain approval of the Philippine assembly's petition. If Sanchez had stopped here, all might be well; unfortunately, he went on to express quite gratuitously his personal opinion of the project itself. It could not possibly succeed, he said…, because whatever might have been the case in apostolic times, experience proved that in the times in which they lived the expansion of Christianity into pagan lands had to have the backing and support of the civil power…" [126]

Sanchez thought that, if he supported Volante, he would be going against God, the King, the Manila Governor and the Bishop and his own conscience, besides causing harm to the Portuguese in Macao and the future of Christianity in China. Times have changed and Volante should not expect that, like the early Apostles who had spread the Christian Gospel without any military escort, his plan would succeed in the 16th century. Could he claim to have a special vocation to go to evangelize China and perhaps die as a martyr, after so many attempts failed to bring Christian faith to that country? This shows that the divine confirmation is missing for such a vocation.

The efforts of Fr. Sanchez in Rome

Fr. Sanchez then left for Rome in Autumn 1588. Pope Sixtus V received him and talked about church affairs in the Philippines and the petitions of Bishop Salazar. Sanchez faithfully and tenaciously submitted a new copy of his report and followed the course of the answer to this issue through

---

[126] H. de la Costa, *The Jesuits in the Philippines* (Cambridge, Mass.: Harvard University Press, 1967), p. 103.

the curia under five different popes, Sixtus V (1585-1590), Urban VII (16-27 September 1590), Gregory XIV (December 1590 - October 1591), Innocent IX (October – December 1591) and Clement VIII (January 1592-1605).

Meanwhile, Fr. Valignano from the Far East kept on worrying about the actions of Fr. Sanchez both in Spain and in Rome. He tried his best to cut any ties that Ruggieri, Ricci and Sanchez had built up among themselves. He not only reacted strongly to the criticism of Fr. Sanchez but also wrote to General Acquaviva in Rome, harshly pointing out the unjustified interference of a Castilian national into the affairs of the Portuguese Indies. In this correspondence, he stressed the importance of proceeding with all due caution in China, in order not to offend the local sensitivity.

"Valignano had no doubt for the Mission in China about making the clear distinction between the missionaries and the European merchants and soldiers. In view of this evaluation, it was of fundamental importance that the Chinese authorities should understand that the Jesuit fathers were subjects of a spiritual sovereign, who would never constitute a military threat to the stability of the Chinese Empire. In view of this, and to counterattack the proposal of a Spanish embassy, he opted for the solution of a papal embassy to the court of Wanli Emperor…

The decision to pursue the idea of a papal embassy focused on Ruggieri for the mission, since probably, in Valignano's opinion, Ruggieri had been wrong to ask for help and advice from Sanchez and had furthermore failed to achieve the chosen goal during his two journeys to the Chinese interior. Ruggieri was certainly somewhat embittered by the poor opinion his superior had of him and his difficult temperament. But on the other hand, he was mild and obedient in nature. Despite being the only person, apart from Ricci, not only to have been permitted to take up residence in China but also to be extremely versed in the Chinese culture, he was now sent back to Europe to examine the possibility of a papal embassy, which would be quite distinct from the policies being pursued by Spain and Portugal. Ruggieri, however, was skeptical of Valignano's strategy and disobeyed the Visitor's orders. He thus arrived in Spain, where he had been expressively forbidden to go and asked to be received by Philip II, who granted him a lengthy audience. From that moment, Ruggieri came down decidedly on the side of the Spanish initiative and made the last leg of his journey to Italy on a vessel belonging to the Duke of Sessa who was going to see Sixtus V and whose express task in going to Rome was to smooth the waters with the Holy See regarding the highly intricate situation in France. During the same period that Ruggieri was in Rome, Sanchez was pushing with the papacy the right of the Spanish king to make a conquest of the East Indies and was received by Acquaviva too who had given him important responsibilities. Thus, Valignano's idea of an autonomous missionary approach in the Far East appeared to be losing ground. But the Spanish policies, despite the enormous power of that nation, did not manage to wear down the Pope's resistance and the death of four popes in rapid succession and the eventual election of the Aldobrandini Clement VIII pushed the affairs of the Far East very much into the place of minor importance." [127]

Pope Gregory XIV, meanwhile, seemed to have solved the debate and taken a decision with three Briefs, whose content unfortunately is known only through the summary made by Fr. Sanchez.[128] They praise the commitment of the Spanish kings to bring the Gospel to the newly discovered pagan lands seem in total favor of the cooperation of the secular forces for the religious enterprise: *"without the military help, neither the preachers, no matter how zealous they are, cannot at last preach the Gospel, nor the pagans who God moves will dare to embrace a Religion so new for them, nor those who have embraced it would return to their errors..."*

Pope Innocent IX praised the efforts and the work of Fr. Sanchez, and Clement VIII renewed to Philip II the gift of Alexander VI and fully approved the work of Fr. Sanchez. But the troubles for the latter were not over.

The Intervention of Bishop Salazar

In late 1591 or early 1592 the news reached him in Rome from Madrid that Fr. Sanchez had been denounced to the king by Bishop Domingo

---

[127] E. Lo Sardo, art. cit., 295-300. D'Elia. In the Introduction to *Fonti Ricciane*, o.c., p. xvii, attributes the merit of the Papal Embassy to China to Fr. Valignano, and put in his mouth the same motivations of Fr. Sanchez in proposing the Spanish Embassy. And he does not speculate on the relationship between Valignano and Ruggieri: "For the project, [Valignano] did not hesitate to sacrifice one of the only two missionaries then living inside China, to send him to Rome with the purpose to obtain and prepare such an embassy".

[128] See H. Bernard, "La Theorie du Protectorat Civil des Missions en Pays Infidèle", in *Nouvelle Revue Theologique*, Mars 1937, pp. 275-276. The three Briefs are *Cum sicuti nuper accepimus in primeval conversione Indor., Insular., Philippinar.* signed by Gregory XIV on 18 April 1591; *Quod in agrorum cultu et proventu segetum frugales coloni facere conserverunt* signed by the nephew of the Pope, Card. Sfrondati on 28 June; *Eximiam potetstatem illam qua cum ab ipsa ineffabilis Verbi Incarnatione praeditus esset Christus salvator noster*, signed by Card. Sfrondati on 28 July, 1591.

138

Salazar as having exceeded his mandate and grossly misrepresented the mind of his superiors, and that his *Razionamento* (Rationale), in particular, ought to be deferred to the Inquisition as savoring heresy.

In fact, Bishop Salazar wrote to the king of Spain asserting that *the ill report concerning the mandarins of China was rather an invention of the Portuguese than a true report.* On June 24, 1590, he has sent another special communication to apologize for having formerly given under mistaken information a wrong impression of the character and attitude of the Chinese toward foreigners, and for having supported the *Empresa de China.*

> *"Under that error I wrote to your Majesty as I felt then; and, although what I wrote was true according to the information received, I have learned since that the contrary is the fact...."*

He blamed the Portuguese for having spread in China false reports about the Chinese hostility. He urged that no unfriendly demonstration should be made against the Chinese, for they were favorable to the Christian religion. He related various cases of their humane treatment of foreigners and of missionaries. He also blamed the calumnies of the Portuguese against the Spaniards for the ill-treatment received by the hands of the Chinese.

> *"... From all the aforesaid we infer that what has been reported of the refusal of the Chinese kingdom, and of its rulers, to permit entrance to foreigners has been invention and slender by the Portuguese, who did this for their own private interests, fearing that their commerce with the Chinese would cease of the Castilians gained entrance there... Therefore, I say that if once I thought it possible to make war to China because of the false report given me of hindrance and obstacles offered by the rulers of that kingdom to the preaching of the gospel, by not allowing those who could preach it to enter the land, now that I know the truth, I declare that one of the worst offenses which could be committed against God and the greatest possible obstacle and opposition to the spread of the gospel, would be to go to China with the mailed hand, or to use any sort of violence..."* [129]
>
> *"When Sanchez learned of the bishop's denunciation, he wrote an apology which he directed to Sebastian Hernandez, one of the Jesuits at Madrid, doubtless with the instructions that it be shown in the proper quarters. Bishop Salazar had urged the king to have the Razionamento examined by the Inquisition. Nothing, says*

---

[129] Blair & Robertson, The Philippine Islands, vol. 7, pp. 212-238. See all these documents in Dr. Manel Olle Rodriguez, *Estrategias filipinas respecto a China: Alonso Sánchez y Domingo Salazar en la empresa de China (1581-1593)*: Barcelona, 1998.

Sanchez, would please him better. Aside from the fact that the doctrine it contained had been approved by many eminent authorities, the bishop himself had defended it on numerous occasions, at the Synod of Manila, in a sermon before the governor and dignitaries of the colony, and at the colonial assembly. In fact, the plan for the expedition to China which was based on that doctrine was drawn up in the bishop's house with the bishop's active participation. The members of the special commission on Philippine affairs to whom the Razionamento was addressed saw nothing wrong with it; on the contrary, they asked Sanchez to put it in writing and furnish them with copies. When he came to Rome, he requested the Spanish ambassador to the Holy See to check his papers, the Razionamento among them, before submitting then to the pope; the ambassador found nothing objectionable in any of them. He personally gave a copy of the Razionamento to Sixtus V, who promised to read it and did read it. But, of course, Sixtus V could not very well disapprove of it because he held the same doctrine himself; he said so. Finally, the cardinals of the Holy Office, to whom his memorials were referred, had every opportunity to examine the Razionamento. Not only did they see nothing wrong with it but their consulted theologian, Francisco de Toledo, told Sanchez that the right delegated by the Holy See to the Spanish crown of compelling a hearing for the Gospel extended even further than Sanchez claimed.

What, then, did Sanchez say in the Razionamento that won so many and such authoritative testimonials? He did not say, as Bishop Salazar apparently thought he said, that ministers of the Gospel cannot and ought not to go into mission territory without an armed escort. What he did say was that they could and might go with such escort, not for aggression but for protection, and that it was often fool-hardly to go without such escort, or to make converts who would be defenseless against persecution for lack of such escort or some sort of civil protectorate.

It should be clear from this that Bishop Salazar, Volante and Sanchez were writing at cross-purposes, for Sanchez never advocated conversions by force, as Salazar and Volante thought he did, nor did Salazar, as Sanchez claimed, approved the armed invasion of China and then denounce both it and him to Philip II. If Salazar changed his mind about the China enterprise it was not because he had abandoned the theory of civil protectorate but because the facts that justified the application of that theory had not, apparently, be correctly reported..."[130]

Sanchez returned to Spain in April 1592 with the powers of 'visitor' in order to fight against the enemies of the Jesuits. He was elected delegate for

---

[130] H. De la Costa, *The Jesuits in the Philippines*, o.c., pp. 103-105.

the general assembly of the Society to be held in Rome in 1593, but, before going, he died on 27 May at Alcala de Nehares.

The results of the Memorial

The time to promote the *Empresa de China* was not the most suitable one. The Spanish economy was in a state of dire crisis and the military situation was equally gloomy. Shortly after the return of Fr. Sanchez to Europe, the defeat of the supposedly *Invincible Armada* destroyed all dreams of a world ruled by the Spanish monarch.

However: "Already in 1596, Philip II had forwarded instructions to the Governor of the Philippines to undertake the conquest of Formosa. But the fleet sent from Manila for this purpose had to return because it met a storm off Mariveles [or Playahonda]" [131]

The atmosphere kept on tense on both Spanish and Chinese sides. In 1595, arrived in Manila many Chinese ships, ostensibly for trade. However, they carried many men and little merchandise, with seven Mandarins bearing the insignia of their office. This led to the suspicion on the part of the Spaniards that the Chinese had heard of the departure of most of the Spanish forces for the Moluccas, and had sent a fleet to try to conquer the nearly defenseless islands. However, seeing the city as strongly defended as ever, the Chinese made no hostile moves. They returned to China without showing any particular motive for the journey.

In 1603, the fact that three Chinese mandarins arrived in Manila to dispense justice among the Chinese, sparked rumors among the Spaniards of an impending Chinese invasion, and a rumor among the Chinese of a Spanish pre-emptive strike to massacre all the Chinese. This led to an uprising. As a consequence of its quelling, Chinese were forced to live outside of the walled city.

---

[131] Pablo Fernandez, OP, *History of the Church in the Philippines, 1521-1898* [Metro Manila: Life Today Publications, 1988], pp. 280-281.

Conclusion

The sense of Mission in the Middle Ages differs from its understanding in the modern era: it was centered upon a concept of 'crusade', coming from the fighting spirit to liberate the Holy Land out of the control of Muslim hands (the spirit of the Crusades and of the 'just war'), and of the conquest of the 'new world' just discovered.

On the contrary,

"we people of the 20ᵗʰ century, so far away in time from these events and from the people who shaped them, find it hard to believe that a handful of Spaniards, laymen and religious alike, could be overcome by these gross imperialistic dreams. The conquest was justified, in their view, because China closed the door to Christianity and to commerce." [132]

Indeed, it is difficult to understand the so-called spirit of conquest and, in particular, *La Empresa de China*. However, the 'colonial dream' should be counterbalanced with the above-mentioned historical records of all the efforts to defend the rights of the local population against the abuses and injustices by the hands of the European colonizers both in the Americas and in the Philippines by courageous and outspoken missionaries.

---

[132] Lucio Gutierrez, "The 'Affair' of China at the end of the 16ᵗʰ Century: Armed Conquest or Peaceful Evangelization?" in A.N. Baxter et alii, eds., *Conference Proceedings of Macao-Philippines Historical Relations* (Macao: Universidade de Macao &CEPESA, 2005), p. 349.

7

THE SURVIVING CHRISTIAN PRESENCE IN CHINA
(XV-XVI centuries)

The common judgment of the historians about the Christian presence in China is that, from the collapse of the Mongols (fall of the Yuan dynasty, in 1368), until the beginning of the Jesuit Mission at the end of the 16th century, when Frs. Michele Ruggieri (1543-1607) e Matteo Ricci (1552-1610) were allowed to take up residence in Zhaoqing, Guangdong (on September 10, 1583), Christianity in China has totally disappeared.

"In the fourteenth and fifteenth centuries, Christianity suffered seemingly disastrous losses in Asia. The far-flung frontiers of the Nestorian churches[133] in China and Central Asia were wiped out and the Christian communities either perished or were assimilated to other faiths [mainly by Islam and Lamaistic Buddhism]. *Roman Catholic missions and the small Christian groups gathered by them in China and Central Asia disappeared. A dwindling Nestorianism survived in Persia, Mesopotamia, and adjoining regions. In several of the cities of Central Asia and India a few Armenian Christians were found, chiefly merchants. In India communities of Nestorians - 'Syrian Christians' - remained. However, Asian Christianity became confined almost entirely to the extreme west of the vast continent."[134]*

During the 15th century, Europe, without any reasonable explanation, gradually forgot almost completely all the detailed information that has been acquired about many countries in Asia. Even the Mongol Empire, that has been a source of fear of all European peoples, was reduced, in the best of cases, just to the name of 'Tartars' and 'Tartaria', whose evangelization some Popes at times were concerned for. The existence of China, known in the Greek and Roman world as 'Sinae' or 'Seres' was forgotten,

---

[133] After the recent studies, scholars more accurately prefer speaking about the "East-Syrian Church", or the "Chaldean Church", "the Church of the East" instead of the Nestorian Church. However, the text of the quotations is kept as it is.

[134] Kenneth Scott Latourette, *A History of Expansion of Christianity* (Grand Rapids, Michigan: Zondervan Publishing House, 1971), vol. 3, p. 3.

confused under different names like Tartaria, Cathay (from the Russian name of the kingdom of Khitan in NW of China, 907-1125) and Manji (South China), according to the names used in Marco Polo's times. The whole Central and East Asia became known as the 'Indies', with very vague boundaries, which included also the eastern coast of Africa. The geographical maps left large empty spaces. However, strange enough, the opinion that somewhere in these 'Indies' continued to exist peoples who were mostly Christian, and a 'Christian country' was led by a 'Christian king-priest' named John, (the legend of the 'Prester John'), descendant of the Wise Kings of Matthew's Gospel, was quite popular. The tradition of the preaching of the Apostle St. Thomas in China was also overspread.

The remnants of the previous evangelization attempts

The origin of the rumor about a previous Christian presence in the northern region of present China, as well as in its central provinces and in the Tibet region, has historical foundation. Indeed, there were lasting traces of the Christian presence in the Chinese Empire and in the neighboring countries.

During the Yuan dynasty and, consequently at the beginning of the Ming dynasty, there lived in China various groups of Christians, namely the Syrian-oriental Christians, the Latin Catholics, converts of the Franciscans, among whom about 30,000 Alans (originally Orthodox, who, in early 14th century, had joined the Catholic Church), Orthodox believers from Hungary, Georgia, Armenia and Russia, as well as followers of Manichaeism. The Mongols used to call Christianity the "Religion of the Cross" (*shizijiao*), and the Christians "adorers of the Cross," while they named all the leaders of the Christian communities *Yelikewen. "the blessed ones"* (probably from the Syrian Arkouna, Persian Arkaoun, Mongol Arkagun[135]). Another general name was *Tie-se* or *Tie-er-sa,* from the Persian *Tersa, "who fears the Lord."*

In the 14th, 15th and 16th centuries, the Syrian Church of the East continued to be concerned and care for its followers living in China from its central headquarters in Bagdad.

---

[135] This name, as we will see, according to Fr. Antoon Mostaert, was inherited by the Mongol clan Erküt.

144

The Franciscan Cathay Vicarage, which was established in 1307 with the appointment of John of Montecorvino (1246-1328) as archbishop of Khanbaliq, covered Eastern Turkestan and China.[136]

After the fall of the Mongol Dynasty in 1368, on March 11, 1370, Pope Urban V sent the French theology professor of Oxford, William of Prat with about 60 friars to Khanbaliq as archbishop.

In 1391, the Franciscans of Khanbaliq sent two friars to ask the Pope for new missionaries. And, again, in 1405, two Franciscans made the journey from Khanbaliq to Rome, while in 1403, it seems that a certain Dominic, succeeded William de Prat, and later Charles of France.

An ancient manuscript dated 1404, *Libellus de Notitia Orbis*, written by John III de Galonifontibus, a French Dominican, who was then archbishop of Sultanieh states:

"In that country there was an archbishop of Khanbaliq, of the Order of Friars Minor, a venerable and saintly man named Charles of France, whose acquaintance I main my younger years. This man lived in those regions and had done much for the spread and glorification of the Faith. Since his death, many years ago, no one has gone to these regions. As a consequence, I myself have been asked repeatedly and I would go there, but I waited for the consent of the Holy See. If it is pleasing to the Most High, I shall move into those parts because we have there a good number of Catholics."[137]

In 1410, the Holy See joined the See of Khanbaliq with the See of Sultanieh, in Persia, under the Dominican archbishop John III; however, bishops of Peking were still nominally appointed up to the year 1475.

In 1405, the Spanish ambassador Ruy Gonzalez de Clavijo saw the arrival at the court of Tamerlane in Samarkand some Christians from Cathay and wrote: "The emperor of Cathay used to be a gentile, but he was converted to the faith of the Christians..." [138]

---

[136] *New Catholic Encyclopedia*, vol. 9, Missions, History of (Medieval).

[137] Bernard H. Willeke, "Did Catholicism in the Yuan Dynasty survive until the present?" in *Tripod*, 47, pp. 67-68.

[138] Ruy Gonzalez de Clavijo, writing in the report of his embassy to Tamerlane in 1404-05, about the city of Samarcand, added: "There was so great a number of people brought to this city, from all parts, both men and women, that they are said to have amounted to one hundred and fifty thousand persons, of many nations, Turks, Arabs, and

Muslims, controlling the routes of Central Asia, impeded all the communication between the Chaldean Christians of North China and the *Catholicos* of Bagdad, but Christians of the southern area of China and probably also of the eastern part could more easily keep contacts with their brethren in Mesopotamia by the sea route.

"The Siro-Malabar Christians, having lost their bishops during long years, have sent delegates in 1490 to the patriarch of Mesopotamia... The Catholicos Mar Simeon appointed for them two bishops, Mar Thomas and Mar John. Mar Thomas afterwards returned to Mesopotamia, where he met Mar Elias the new Catholicos. The latter consecrated three new bishops for the Siro-Malabar Christianities: Mar Yahb Alaha, Mar Denis and Mar Jacob who returned with Mar Thomas to Malabar. From there, the fours bishops sent an interesting letter, dated from India in 1504, and through it we are informed that they are appointed also for the islands located between Dagab and Sin and Masin". [139]

Dagab was Java, Sin and Masin, China and the southern region of China. In fact, about the year 1508, a Syrian priest, known under the name of Josephus Indus, went to Rome in pilgrimage together with his brother Matthew, and informed that the Indians and inhabitants of the Cathay were Christians, with the Catholicos sending bishops in those countries.

Quite a few of Orthodox believers, as well as the Alans, many of whom were converted to the Catholic Church by Montecorvino, continued to live in China under the Ming Dynasty: this fact has been certified by the research of Henry Serruys, a specialist in Mongol history and affairs. He, in

---

Moors, Christian Armenians, Greek Catholics, and Jacobites, and those who baptize with fire in the face, who are Christians with peculiar opinions. There was such a multitude of these people that the city was not large enough to hold them, and it was wonderful that a number lived under trees, and in caves... Fifteen-day journey from the city of Samarcand, in the direction of China, there is a land inhabited by Amazons, and to this day they continue the custom of having no men with them, except at one time of the year... These women are subject to Timour Beg; they used to be under the emperor of Cathay, and they are Christians of the Greek Church." (see Google Books, Narrative of the Embassy of Ruy Gonzalez. pdf)

[139] A Syrian document, dated 1504, located in the Vatican [Vat. Syr. 204], translated by A. Mingana, reported by S.H. Moffet, *A History of Christianity in Asia*, Vol. I (San Francisco: Harper, 1992), p. 502.

an article on "*The Mongols in China during the Hungwu period (1368-1398)*", demonstrates that "with the fall of the Yuan Empire not all Mongols (and their inner Asian allies) left China. Large numbers, no doubt many of them born in China, never left the country and passed under Chinese control: being most of them soldiers of long standing, they came to be incorporated in the army of the new rulers."[140]

In another article, *"Mongols in China: 1400-1450"*, the same author concluded: "If indeed the Mongols and Central Asians were so numerous at the Chinese capital [during the Ming dynasty] as these cases suggest, one may wonder where they came from. It is quite possible that they were remnants of the Mongol forces of the Yuan dynasty, who had remained in China after 1368. As it has already been indicated, the fact is that after 1400 a variety of factors such as famine, civil wars, etc., and perhaps most of all the appeal of a superior civilization, prompted many Mongols to seek admittance to China..."[141]

Consequently, it was quite possible that the Catholic Alans, who were employed as imperial guards under the Mongols, could have continued their work and presence in China. The same could possibly have happened to other Catholic and Orthodox believers.

It was around 1505-1506 that Lodovico da Barthema (Varthema c. 1470-1517) of Bologna who, in his travels from 1502–1510, met Chinese Christian merchants in Bengal and with them visited other places in South East Asia departing from them in Melika (Malacca, Malaysia). They told him that "in their country there were many rich people, also Christian, but they were under the Great Khan of the Cathay... And these men were white as us, and confess to be Christian, and believe in the Trinity, as well as in the Twelve Apostles, in the Evangelists, and have also the baptism in water; but they write differently from us, that is in the Armenian way. They said to believe in the birth and passion of Christ, to keep our Lent and many vigils during the year..."[142]

In 1546, when in Malacca, St. Francis Xavier, met a Portuguese merchant from China who told that on some mountains of China live a group

---

[140] In *Mélanges Chinois et Buddhiques*, vol. 11, 1959.
[141] In *Monumenta Serica*, XXVII, 1968, p. 250.
[142] www.e-text.it Ramusio G.B. Navigazioni e viaggi.

of people, isolated from the rest, who, though they are not Muslims, do not eat pork and celebrate many festivities.[143]

The Spanish Dominican friar, Gaspar da Cruz, who stayed in Guangzhou towards the end of 1556, in his book confirmed the presence of Tartars and Alans in the Ming army:

"…In the city of Cantam [Canton, present Guangzhou] I saw many Tartar captives who have no other captivity than to serve for men-at-arms in other places far from Tartary; and they wear, for a difference, red caps, being otherwise dressed like the Chinese with whom they live. They have for their maintenance a certain stipend of the King, which they have paid them without fail. The Chinese call them Tatas, for they cannot pronounce the letter r… The Chinas say that the King of China has many men of war in pay, who do keep the weak passes and the walls on the side of the Tartars. They say that they are great men with great beards, and wear cut-hose and caps and blunt swords. And a Portugal that was carried captive the land inward, told me that he had heard the Chinese say that they called these men Alimenes"[144]

Related to his experience, Gaspar da Cruz wrote:

"When I was in the region of the Apostle saint Thomas suffered martyrdom, which the Portuguese call Sao Thomé and those of the country Moleapor [Mylapore], I learned that an honorable Armenian had come thither on a pilgrimage from Armenia out of devotion to the Apostle, and he deposed on oath that the Armenians had it written in their true and authentic scriptures that before the Apostle suffered martyrdom a Moleapor he had gone to China to preach the Gospel, after being there certain days, seeing that he could not do any good there, he had returned to Moleapor, leaving in China three or four disciples who he had made there, - all of which was set down in the book of the house. If these disciples whom the Apostle had left, had made fruit in the land, and through them the land came to the knowledge of God, we do not know it; for generally among them there is no notice of the evangelical law, nor of Christianity, nor even of One God, nor a trace thereof…

In the city of Canton in the midst of the river which is of fresh water and very broad, is a little islet on which is a kind of monastery of their sort of priests; and within this

---

[143] See his report, p. 44.

[144] Gaspar da Cruz, *Treatise in which the things of China are related at great length, with their particularities, as likewise of the Kingdom of Ormuz, 1569*, in C.R. Boxer, *South China in the Sixteenth Century… o.c.*, pp. 85-86. "Almayne, and Alimenes", is understood by both Gaspar da Cruz and C.R. Boxer as Allemande and Almains (Germany), but it seems more probable to refer it to the 'Alans'.

monastery I saw an oratory high from the ground very well made, with certain gilt steps before it, made of carved work, in which was a woman very well made with a child about her neck, and it had a lamp burning before it. I suspecting that to be some show of Christianity, asked of some laymen whom I found there, and of some idol's priests who were there, what that woman signified, and none could tell it me, nor give me any reason for it. It might well be the image of Our Lady, made by ancient Christians that Saint Thomas left there, or by their occasion made, but the conclusion is that all is forgotten. It might also be some heathen image."[145]

Sporadic presence

Other sporadic presence of Christians was found. Merchants and travelers continued to enter China. The Portuguese first arrival to the China coasts at the island of Tamão, in 1513, was followed by many attempts to enter the Chinese Empire and to send embassies to the emperor. As we have seen, the Chinese authorities became worried about their activities and ordered to eliminate them and put into prison the foreigners who were caught. In the battles at Tamão and Xicaowan in 1521 and 1522, and those of Ningbo and Xiamen Bay in 1548 and 1549, Chinese made a good number of Portuguese prisoners.

Moreover, several of Portuguese and Spanish trips to China turned into tragedies due to natural storms or bad encounters with pirates. Due to shipwrecks on Chinese shores, several people found themselves stranded in these lands. Episodes of such people who found themselves for one reason or another living in China and spreading their Christian faith have been recorded by Fr. Marcelo de Ribadeneira in his *"Historia de la Islas del Arcipelago Filippino y Reinos de la Gran China, Tartaria, Cochinchina, Malaca, Siam, Cambodge y Japon"*, written in 1598.[146] The chapter 8 of this book reports some episodes of this kind, whose truthfulness, however, cannot be certified.

---

[145] His "Treatise...", reported in C.R. Boxer, *South China...*, o. c., p. 213.

[146] Fr. Marcelo de Ribadeneira arrived in Manila in May 1594, left for Japan in the following August, and returned to Manila in January 1598 via Macao. He went back to Madrid in 1600. The book was written in 1598, published in 1601, re-published by La Editorial Catolica of Madrid in 1947, according to the original edition.

"Among other books kept by the Chinese, there is one entitled Toxefalen [sic], which reports that, having entered the city of Colozan a man named Mateo Escandel, Hungarian native of the city of Buda, who has been hermit on Mount Sinai and had come there as a merchant of the king of Siam, he not only was leading a very hard life, but worked many miracles in the name of God Our Lord. And having brought again to life five dead persons, his holiness became known and much venerated by the ordinary people of that city. The priests of the idols, proclaiming him a sorcerer, wanted to unmask and win him in public debates. But in the first and all other debates, they were won by the holy man, who gave witness to the truth of the law of God. Therefore, afraid of their reputation, they incited the whole population, threatening them: a fire from heaven will descend and burn the city if they should not get rid of that sorcerer and impostor. A crowd of idolaters, so excited by the envy of their priests, gathered at the residence of the servant of God. And as soon as his guest, named Joane, went to meet the infuriated crowd, he was killed with his son and sons-in law in defense of the saint. The latter, full of courage, face the public and rebuking the demonstrators of their sins, announced the true Savior, our Lord Jesus Christ... and since this cut the obstinate priests to the quick, they incited the furious mob... and hit him with poles to death. They threw the corpse down the river, but the current kept it for five days, at the sight of whole people, several of whom repented. At the end they could not help but bury him. After the burial, the whole city shook so much that many ran way on the mount. The priests, fearing the heavenly punishment, gathered the whole night in the temple with a following of four thousand colleagues to beg their gods to stop the earthquake. But in vain: the temple collapsed upon them, the earth opened up and buried them alive. The hole created by the earthquake became a lake and the city, which was called in the local language City of Flower, is called now Punishment of Heaven. What is left is only ruins as sign of its former greatness as well as a village named Xifagan, where when the Portuguese arrived, they found some faithful who knew this sentence: "Jesus Christ, Mary always Virgin conceived Him, Virgin delivered Him and Virgin remains". And getting to know that they were Portuguese of the same faith, reported to them the details of such a marvelous case and showed them a book of the marvels of the Lord worked thought his servant.
Likewise, in the city of Sampitay, the Portuguese came across with some other Christians, converted by the good example of life and the holy words of a daughter of a Portuguese, named Ines,[147] *who lived there. Since her father (as she referred), called Tomé Pires, has been left in that city, he got married with her Chinese*

---

[147] The episode of the meeting with Ines de Leyria is described also by Hernandez M. Pinto in his "Peregrinations" (*Peregrinação*) with a longer text. According to some commentators, the lady should be a Eurasian woman who had earlier been converted to Christianity by Portuguese.

150

mother and converted her to the Christian faith; having lived there for twenty-seven years, he baptized many people and taught them whatever doctrine he knew. After the death of her father, this blessed woman kept in her house a chapel, in secret, clean and decorated with a great cross and candlesticks, all gilded. And more than three hundred Christians who lived nearby gathered together on Sundays, and kneeling down with the hands and the eyes raised to heaven all together prayed: "Lord Jesus Christ, since it is true that you are the true Son of God, conceived by the power of the Holy Spirit in the womb of the Virgin Holy Mary, for the salvation of the sinners, forgive our sins, so that we can merit the glory of your kingdom, where you are seated at the right hand of the supreme Father of ours, who is in heaven and whose name be sanctified. In the name of the Father, and of the Son and of the Holy Spirit. Amen". After having recited this short but substantial prayer, since they did not know much, they kissed the cross and embrace one another with fraternal charity and then return to their homes and all lived in great peace and brotherhood. The reason for not knowing many prayers was due to the fact that the book that contained many prayers was taken away by the pagans. So, in gratitude for the kindness showed by this good Christian to the Portuguese, they wrote down the whole Christian Doctrine and other holy prayers. And on leaving, they gave her some financial subsidy…

The same nine Portuguese, who toured the Great China for twenty years (as I find according to their report to the cardinal prince when was ruling Portugal) refer that in another city, called Quansi, during a tour of one of them, without paying attention to what was happening, he met with an old man, dressed in black silk interwoven with white leather threads, who on the side of the path made him signs as for calling him. Thinking that he was a kind of thief, the Portuguese wanted to get away, but the old man called him and showed him a cross of silver, which he kept on his neck. The old man, then approached him and kneeling at his feet said in Portuguese: "Praise be the Most Sweet Name of Our Lord Jesus Christ, since at the end of many years of exile, allowed my eyes to see a Spaniard who professes the law of my God put on a cross". And the Portuguese, shaken by what he was seeing and hearing, asked him: "On the part of our Lord Jesus Christ I order you to tell me who you are". Then, the old man crying abundantly answered: "I am Portuguese and my name is Vasco Calvo; it is more than twenty-seven years that I was lost in this land, where I was taken prisoner". And talking about his brothers and relatives, the Portuguese, with no little emotion, embraced him as a brother in faith and in nationality. And he made account of the other companions; then all went to his house to meet his wife, kids and daughters, who were serving God among the pagans. The wife led them the chapel located in a secret place, kept with great decorum with a great cross and two candlesticks of silver, as well as with a lamp. The whole family of the old man knelt down and prayed with great devotion in Portuguese.

*They recited a special prayer, followed by the Pater Noster, Ave Maria, Credo and
Salve Regina in the same language, pronounced most properly, with great admira-
tion of the guests who were moved to tears. They separated, promising each other
mutual prayer.*

*And the writer concludes warning everybody to pray and offer sacrifices for "those
faithful who live among idolaters, who must be numerous in those lands, since the
shipwrecks are quite frequent in the kingdoms and provinces of the gentiles. So that
the Lord keep them in His holy faith and love and give them a holy death and,
after it, the eternal beatitude".*

In 1575, in his journey to Fujian, Fr. Martin Rada met a few Christians
in Fuzhou.

*"They found a few Christians in Hochin [Fujian], something which gave Rada im-
measurable joy. These Christians told him that they had received the faith from the
Portuguese, particularly those who had lived in the city of Hiucha and at the sea
port. Rada mentions the names of two of them: Hieronimo and Francisco Pedro.
He encouraged them to keep alive the spirit of faith they had received; they answered
they would do so, but that 'because of fear they tried not to be found out'."*[148]

Matteo Ricci's search for the "adorers of the cross" in China

Fr. Alvarez Semedo (1567-1658), one of the earliest Portuguese Jesuits
in China and author of *The History of China* (1655), wrote that they could
not find any trace of the ancient Christians: "It is true we found a small
bell, such as is used at Mass, with Greek letters round about it, and a cross
very handsomely graved."[149]

However, the twinkling of this bell, together with other traces and rev-
elations from various parts, set up Fr. Matteo Ricci in search for the 'lost
Christians'.

---

[148] Pedro G. Galende, *Apologia Pro Filipinos* (Salesiana Publishers, Manila, 1980), p.
191.

[149] Quoted in C. Cary-Elwes, *China and the Cross* (New York: Kennedy & Sons, 1957),
p. 71. The news is taken from the record and letters of Fr. Ricci (see. D'Elia, *Fonti Ricciane*,
o.c., vol. I, no. 173.

In letters dated July 26, 1605, and November 12, 1607, from Beijing, the father informed that some traces of Christianity could be found in various provinces. Probably he did not know the above quoted news of St. Francis Xavier. However, Fr. Ricci based his statement upon a visit he received in 1605 by a Jew, Ngai (Ai) Tian, who informed him about the presence of the Jews in China, mainly in Zhejiang, Shanxi and a dozen of families in Kaifeng, Henan, with a synagogue, which possessed a copy of the five rolls of the Pentateuch. He was also informed about the presence in Kaifeng of "adorers of the cross": *Although this religion is extinct, yet the Jew said that many kept this custom of making the cross, and were known by their look which was quite different from that of other persons.*

On July 26, 1605, Fr. Ricci gave more details to the Superior General, Fr. Claudio Acquaviva:

"A few days ago, we came to know for certain that there have been a good number of Christians in China for the past five hundred years, and that there are still considerable traces of them in many places. Of recent years I have written that we have found a community in lands subject to China but outside the great northern walls, where to this day, for want of a few 'scuti' [escudos] to make the journey there, we have sent no one to find out how many they are or whence they came. Now we know that in the middle of China, half a month from here and the same distance from Nan-ching, in the province of Ho-nan and in the capital which is called Kaifeng-fu there are five or six families of Christians who have now lost almost all the little Christianity they had, because several years ago they turned the church into the temple of an idol called Kuan Wang. What has hindered us from knowing of them until now is that they are not called by the name of Christians but by their race of Tersa, which seems to be the name of the country from which they came to China, and by the religion of 'shih tzu' (shizi), which means 'of the figure of ten' which in Chinese writing is a perfect cross like this + ; for in appearance and features and in not worshipping idols they were like the Moors and Jews and were only distinguished by the fact that they ate pork and all kinds of flesh, making over it a cross with the hand. We learnt this from a Jew in religion, race, and features, who came to see me the other day due to the fame he heard and due to a book printed about many of our things: understanding that we were neither Moors nor Gentiles, he considered us belong to his own law. The surname of this man is (Ng)ai of the Henan province, but living in the capital...

The next day the Jew brought to our house a fellow countryman of his named Chang, who he said was a descendant of the Christians, who also had to obtain office and had received a post in the province of Shan-hsi [Shanxi] near to those an-

cient Christians outside the walls, who are subject to him by virtue of this new office. With this man we made great friends and he showed a great wish to understand all about our religion and to return to the religion of his forefathers. But in six days he left Peking and was always very busy, besides the obstacle, which he had in polygamy. And so, he left, to settle this in another time. But he promised to do his best in both places, that is his home and, in the place, where he holds office, to find out how much was still left of Christianity and, what I wanted more, what writing they used, whether Syriac or, as it seems more likely, Greek: as I am inclined to think by a bell which I saw ten years ago in the hands of a Chinaman. It was very old and had crosses and Greek letters on it and came, it seems, from that country of Ho-nan... "[150]

In 1607 Fr. Ricci sent a Chinese brother, Anthony Leitao, to Kaifeng to verify the information: he confirmed the fact that several families have remained Christian until about the middle of the previous century. The reason for hiding themselves, most probably, was the accusation of having cooperated with the Mongols, who around the year 1550 have made an incursion reaching even Beijing.

From these and other sources, Fr. Ricci got other details about the "adorers of the cross": he was given the names of all the families in Henan who were descended from these people. Among them there was a *shang-shu* (president) of a Board of Revenue at Nanjing, named Chang (Zhang), and other officials; for in the days when this religion was flourishing, they had all been persons of great influence and military prowess. They used to recite prayers from the 'Jewish scriptures', that is from the Psalter; over everything which they ate or drank they made a cross with their finger. According to what he has heard from other Jesuits, in many places in China to make a black cross on the forehead of little children to defend them from all misfortune; and this was the reason why people were suspicious of them. Since their appearance was sufficiently unlike that of the Chinese, they were called *hui-hui* like the Saracens and Jews, except that people called these descendants of the Christians *shih-tzu hui-hui (shizi huihui)*, which means 'Saracens of the Cross'.[151]

---

[150] Quoted by A.C. Moule, *Christianity in China before the Year 1500* (London 1930), pp.7-9; F. D'Arelli (ed.), *Lettere (1580-1609) Matteo Ricci,* (Quadeni Quodlibet, Macerata, 2001), pp. 412-415.

[151] A.C. Moule, Christianity in China before the Year 1500, o. c., pp. 4-5. Ricci > Acquaviva 8 March 1608 in F. D'Arelli, *Lettere Matteo Ricci…* o.c., p. 470, where he deals

Fr. Ricci wrote:

"Few years ago, we came to know that certainly there were also Christians, especially in these northern provinces, under the name of 'adorers of the Cross'. They so flourished that they increased not only in the number of families, but also in success in letters and in army, to a certain extent that the Chinese became suspicious, pushed on the line by Muslims who everywhere are our enemies. Consequently, they planned to catch them. So, they were forced to hide themselves, gradually becoming Turks and, by the majority, Gentiles; their churches were turned into temples of idols. And their descendants, although they still keep the tradition of making the sign of the cross upon the food they eat and drink, remained with so great a fear that they do not want to confess to be their descendants. Nobody, neither among them nor among others, know the reason of making the crosses. But their physical features clearly show that they are children of foreign people in China." [152]

In 1613 Fr. Julius Aleni (1582-1649) could go to Kaifeng to visit the Jewish synagogue, but he was not shown the rolls of the Pentateuch. Later, Fr. Nicholaus Trigault (1577-16228) who reached China soon after Fr. Ricci's death in 1610, reported of numerous Christians in North China.

The discovery of the *Jingjiaobei*, the so-called 'Nestorian Stele' and the translation of its text, in 1623-25, confirmed, beyond all doubts, a previous Christian presence in China in the 7th and 8th century. But, at the same time, it raised the question about their disappearance.

In 1645, the Jesuits found traces of their presence: they discovered two Syrian churches in Chongan, in Fujian, although without Christian community, which were considered dated back to the Tang dynasty.[153]

Bento de Goes and the search for Christians in Cathay

As it has been already mentioned in the appendix of chapter 5, in India, many years before the end of 16th century, king and people have heard that

---

also with the journey of Bro. Fr. Benedetto de Goes, as well as in the letter to the same dated August 22, 1608).

[152] D'Elia, *Fonti Ricciane*, o.c. vol. I, no. 173.

[153] Joseph Dehergne, "Les Chretientés de Chine de la période Ming (1581-1650)", in *Monumenta Serica*, XVI, 1957, p. 36.

the Emperor of Cathay was a Christian, and many of his people were Christians. Andrea Corsali (1487-?) on January 6, 1515, from Cochin informed Giuliano de' Medici of Florence that merchants from China were trading in Melaka and added: "I believe that they are Gentiles, although many say that they observe our faith, or at least part of them".[154] The Jesuit missionaries, who followed the arrival in India of St. Francis Xavier in May 1542 (at the time of his death in 1552, there were 64 Jesuits in India), soon heard rumors about Christians living in Cathay and somewhere beyond the Himalaya Mountains, and naturally they were eager to explore the area and to make contact with these supposed co-religionists.

"Although at this time [towards the end of the 16th century], *the Fathers of India had received the news that China was the same as Cathay and it was clear to them, however some doubts were raised by the saying of the Saracens that in the Cathay many, if not all, were Christians, while the* [Jesuit] *Fathers in China said that there were none and the Christian faith has never been introduced there; consequently, that there should be another kingdom of Cathay, near that of China, from which also part of China, gets the name…"* [155]

In 1579, the Mogul ruler of North India, Emperor Akbar (1542-1605, r. 1556-1605), invited "two learned priests" at his court. The invitation elicited great hopes among the Jesuits in Goa. The Provincial, Fr. Rui Vicente chose three Jesuits for the project. They were Fr. Rodolfo Acquaviva, Italian from Naples, who led the mission, Fr. Antonio Monserrate, Portuguese, and the Persian born Bro. Francis Henriques as their companions. They were warmly welcomed by Akbar who wanted to learn about the Christian religion and Western art. They stayed at the court for three years, hoping in vain to convert the emperor. During their stay, they got news about a new nation called 'Bottan' (in India, Tibet was called 'Bhotanta', Tibetan, Bod). Fr. Monserrate wrote, in his "Commentary of the Legation at the Mogul": [156]

------

[154] www.e-text.it (Ramusio G.B., Navigazioni e viaggi).

[155] *Fonti Ricciane*, vol. II, pp. 396-397.

[156] Quoted by Giuseppe Toscano, *La Prima Missione Cattolica nel Tibet* (Parma: Istituto Missioni Estere Parma: Hong Kong, Nazareth Press, 1951) pp. 12-14.

Anyway, when some of these Yogis (sages) were asked by the Jesuits about the mountainous region of Himalaya, they answered that the mountain chain is very high and difficult to climb, but, once its top is reached, it becomes plain and habitable and that in the very ancient city of Manasarovar, there was a people who every eight days gather together to pray and offer a sacrifice of bread and wine. The Jesuits wanted to certify this information but various events prevented them to send somebody there.

In 1591, a second mission to Mogul Akbar, consisting of Fr. Edward Leitao, Fr. Christopher de Vega and Bro. Stephen Riberio arrived at Lahore at the emperor's invitation. But it lasted less than a year. On their advice, in January 1592, Pope Clement VIII wrote a letter to Emperor Akbar, inviting him to learn and follow the Christian faith and to listen to the Jesuit fathers.[157] In May 1595, Akbar made a third invitation: Fr. Jerome Xavier (1549-1617, grandnephew of St. Francis Xavier) accompanied by Fr. Manuel Pinheiro and Brother Bento de Goes (Benedict de Gois, 1562-1607) arrived in Lahore. This time, Akbar gave them permission to open a school and to build churches at Agra and Lahore. He commissioned Fr. Xavier to translate the life of Christ into Persian, work, which was completed in 1602. It was in one of the trips to Kashmir with the ruler that Fr. Xavier and Bro. Bento heard about the presence of Christians, bishops and priests living in the country called Tebat. They soon sent letters in Por-

---

[157] See *Bullarium Romanun*, anno 1592, pp. 646-647,

tuguese and Persian to them. In his correspondence to Rome, Fr. Xavier gives news about the kingdom of Tebat, located in the eastern side of the "*Shetaium vel Cataium*" [Xatai or Cathay], where there is that extraordinary and famous wall of three hundred miles, which divides and separates Tartaria from Sina."[158] Back in Lahore, Fr. Xavier could get further information from a Muslim merchant about "the kingdom of Xatai". He wrote to Rome:

"One day, while I was chatting with the Prince, a sixty-year-old Muslim merchant arrived. Asked by the Prince from where he was coming and by which way, he answered that he was coming from the kingdom of Xatai, via Mecca. Requested about the things in Xatai, he answered that he has lived in that kingdom for 13 years, in the city of the king's residence, called Xabalu, that is our Cambalu… As far as religion is concerned, he said that there are 'Isauites', that is, followers of Jesus: so, they call Christians from the name of Jesus, and not from Christ as we do. There are also many 'Mussauites' that is, Jews (followers of Mussa, Moses) and moreover, there are many Muslims… He stated that they are Christians and with some of them he became friend. They have many churches – he continued; - some of them magnificent for their greatness; they also keep images, both painted and engraved, especially of Crucifixes, and everybody venerate them with great devotion and give offerings… The priests lead a celibate life, run schools and educate children, preparing them for the sacred offices, all supported by the king. The king builds churches and repairs those in bad state… He said that he has often seen the king going to the church, since he is Christian. There are also many people of both sexes who profess a celibate life, almost monastic, and keep in places not attended by the common people. Others keep celibacy at home, in their private houses…" [159]

Consequently, both Akbar and the Jesuits wanted to clarify the enigma about the presence of Christians in Cathay, as well as to certify whether or not Cathay should be identified with China. In fact, they were receiving news from their confreres, together with the opinion of Fr. Matteo Ricci that Cathay should be identified with China.

They were aware of the existence of a route from India to Cathay through Central Asia, since Muslim merchants have traveled to and from Khanbaliq, the capital of Cathay. Therefore, they in agreement with Akbar decided to send a delegation, led by Brother Bento de Goes with the double

---

[158] G. Toscano, *La prima Missione…*, o.c., p. 19.
[159] Id., pp. 21-22.

158

mission. Bento was a native of Villa Franca do Campo (o San Miguel) in the Azores islands. As a soldier in India, he had visited a chapel along the Travancore coast and decided to enter the Society of Jesus as a simple Brother. He studied Persian and, as we have seen, accompanied Fr. Jerome Xavier to the court of the Mogul ruler.

With letters of introduction from Akbar, Bento, dressed as an Armenian merchant, with some companions joined a caravan that left Agra in October 1602, crossed the Hindustan until Peshawar. Then, he entered the present Afghanistan, and passing through Kabul, he went north in order to cross the mountain chain of Hindukush. Then, he descended into Badakhshan, and turning East he crossed the Pamir reaching Yarkand, in western Xinjiang, which was then the capital of the kingdom of Kashgar. From there he made a detour to Hotan to get back money he had landed to the local queen. Then, with a new caravan, he followed the ancient Silk Road, reaching Maral-bashi, Aksu and Kucha in November 1604. At Yen-ch'i he met a Muslim merchant who had lived with Matteo Ricci in the quarters for foreigners in Khanbaliq. So, Bento became convinced that Cathay and China were identical. With his faithful servant he continued the journey touching Turfan and Hami and crossed the Great Wall at Jiuyuguan. Then, he reached Suchow, in Gansu, in late 1605, where he remained waiting for the possibility to reach Beijing. Meanwhile, he wrote few letters to Fr. Ricci. In reply, Ricci sent a Jesuit brother, John Fernandes, Chung Ming-li, who could speak Portuguese. Bro. John arrived to Suchow less than two weeks before Goes died. When Bento received the letters from Fr. Ricci, kissed and kept them on his heart for the whole night, advising the brother to inform Fr. Ricci that he did not meet any Christian on his way, and that nobody else should be asked to make that journey due to the many difficulties he encountered, as well as assuring that Cathay is nothing else but China.

Bento has met no Christian. However, when he was staying in Yarkand, the king of Kashgar showed him manuscripts well decorated and written in red and round characters, which were dealing with the mystery of the Holy Trinity.[160] Moreover, the account of the mission notes:

---

[160] Quoted by Henri Bernard, *La Découverte de Nestoriens Mongols aux Ordo set l'Histoire ancienne du Christainisme en Estreme-Orient* (Haute Etudes, Tientsin, 1935), pp. 11-12.

"When he arrived at Chalis [facing Karashar] and went to the palace of the ruler of the land, he was asked to debate with some Muslim masters of the law. The Brother explained with so clear and convincing proofs the truth of the Christian faith, that they could not answer. The local ruler supported the position of our party, approving and agreeing with what the Brother was saying and, at the end, he concluded that Christians are the true 'Miserman' (Muslims), which means for the Saracens 'faithful or of the true religion', and added that his ancestors too have been Christians." [161]

"Bento de Goes has met at Qarashar, at the beginning of the 17th century, some Mongols who believed to recognize in the faith he was preaching the same doctrine that their ancestors had followed. The same must have been for the 'Asud' in the Ming dynasty, who, due to the identity of the name, should have been the descendants of the As (Az) or Alans of the Mongol epoch, and these were not only Christian but Orthodox Christian…" [162]

The search for Christians in Tibet

About the news of the existence of Christians beyond the Himalayan Mountains, the initiative was taken again by the Jesuits in India some years later. It was Fr. Antonio De Andrade, who decided to take action: *"We had already gathered with great diligence and from various sources numerous information indicating that in those regions there were Christian kingdoms. These voices continually, from twenty years ago until now, reached our fathers."* [163]

De Andrade was born in Oleiros, Portugal in 1580, entered the Society of Jesus on December 15, 1595, and four years later was sent to India, where after missionary work at the Jesuit colleges at Goa he was appointed head of all the missionary stations in the territories of the Great Mogul of Hindustan. In the spring of 1624, while in Delhi, Andrade came to know that a large group of Hindu travelers were just about to depart on a pilgrimage to a famous temple somewhere on the Himalaya Mountains. An-

---

[161] D'Elia, *Fonti Ricciane*, o.c., vol. II, p. 425 (no. 829).

[162] M. Pelliot, *Revue des Arts asiatiques*, tome 7, 1931, p. 13, quoted by H. Bernard, *La Découverte de Nestoriens Mongols…*, o.c., p. 50.

[163] Andrade > Provincial, November 8, 1624 from Agra, published in Lisboa in 1626 with the title "Novo Descobrimento do Gram Cathayo ou Reinos de Tibet", reported by G. Toscano, *La prima Missione…*, o.c., pp. 49-76.

drade and a Jesuit companion, Manuel Marques, both disguised as Hindus, left from Delhi with the pilgrim caravan in early April 1624. On the way up the valley of the Ganges River, their disguise failed and they were stopped as spies. Eventually released for lack of evidence, the Jesuits rejoined the caravan, but were soon detained again. Finally, they admitted that they were on a mission to reach Tibet. At first, the authorities adamantly refused to let them proceed, but later let them go on. At the beginning of June, the caravan, with Andrade and Marques, reached their destination, the sacred shrine of Badrinath in the Himalayas. Badrinath, of course, was not Andrade's goal. By himself he probed north to the village of Mana, where Andrade encountered traders from the land of Bhot, and from them gathered information on the route. Back in Badrinath, Andrade was then informed that the local ruler, the Rajah of Srinagar (Serinangar, capital of Garhwal, small kingdom tributary of the Mogul) had expressly forbidden him to proceed to Tibet. But he, hoping to be able to enter within eight days in the court of the king of Tibet ("where – he wrote – we have new infallible news that there are many and very good Christians" [164]) decided to ignore this prohibition and to sneak into the country. With two servants from Mana - Marques stayed behind - he pushed on, even though it was the wrong season to cross the pass and heavy snow could be expected. They reached Mana pass. The immense plateau of Tibet was spread out tantalizingly before the trio. They probably would have perished from frostbite and exposure had they not encountered after three days march a Tibetan, who had been sent to check on their whereabouts by the people of Mana. After other few days, the party camped in some caves, where they were joined by a caravan with Manuel Marques, who had brought forward some much-needed provisions.

There, while waiting for the weather to improve, they were met by two guards sent by the king of Tibet who had been informed of their arrival, with the invitation to visit him. So, Andrade could finally set foot in the town of Tsaparang, on the banks of the Langchen Khambab River, sometime around early August 1624. At first, the king was not thrilled to discover that Andrade was not a trader of pearls and jewels but the representative of a religion other than the Buddhism. But after Andrade ex-

---

[164] Letter of Andrade dated May 16, 1624, from Serinangar, quoted by G. Toscano, *La prima Missione…*, o.c., p. 4).

plained that he had come to search for his co-religionists who were believed to be living somewhere in Tibet, the king, who was himself a deeply religious man, relented. He was impressed by the fact that Andrade had risked his life on such a mission. He gradually came to enjoy Andrade's company so much that eventually he forbade him to leave until he promised to return the following year. He also authorized the construction of a Christian "house of prayer" in Tsaparang and furnished Andrade with a pass which read in part:

> *"We the King of the Kingdoms of Potente, rejoice at the arrival in our lands of Fr. Antonio Frangim* [Faringi o Ferangi, the name for all foreigners coming from the West] *to teach us the holy law. We take him for our superior teacher and give him full authority to teach our people. We shall not allow anyone to molest him in this, and will provide him with a 'house of prayer…"*

Armed with the king's approbation, Andrade's passage back to Mana proceeded without incident, and after some delays, he moved on to Jesuit headquarters in Agra, where he arrived the first week of November 1624. On November 8, he began work on his account of the expedition, *Novo Descobrimento do gram Cathayo, ou Reinos de Tibet, pelo Padre Antonio de Andrade da Companhia de Jesu, Portuguez, no anno de 1626,* published in Lisbon in 1626. Andrade was apparently the first European to enter Tibet from India and leave a record of his journey.

Andrade made good on his promise to return to Tsaparang. He left Agra on June 17, 1625 and arrived in Tsaparang on August 28. From Chinese traders who arrived in Tsaparang with tea, porcelain, and other merchandize, Andrade learned more about the geography of the immense "roof of the world": "the kingdom of Potente or Tibet" he later wrote, "comprised numerous small kingdoms, including the kingdom of Guge, of which Tsaparang was the capital, and the kingdom of Utsang, one and a half month's journey to the east." He also got the impression that these various kingdoms, along with "the great empire of Sopo [Mongolia], which borders on China on one side and one Moscovia on the other."

In none of the kingdoms of Tibet, Andrade also learned, were any Christians, the search for which had been the original motivation of his expeditions. The absence of Christians, of course, did not stop from Andrade from proselytizing. The king kept his promise of constructing a "prayer house" for the missionaries and on Easter Day, April 12, 1626, the cornerstone was laid for the first Christian church in Tibet.

Fr. De Andrade was soon followed by other Jesuits, the Portuguese Frs. Stephen Cacella (1585-1630) and John Cabral (1599-1669), who in 1626 from Bengal reached and stayed for some time in Shigatse. Probably in the spring 1630, Fr. Andrade was called back to Goa as Provincial and there he died on March 19, 1634. In 1633 there were five Jesuits in Tibet. However, by the late 1630s the mission has been abandoned.

Recent discoveries

Some very vague traditions can be mentioned about the 'survival' of the Christian presence in China, concerning the Buddhist monasteries of Hangzhou, Zhejiang, which could have Franciscan origin, traditions which lasted until the 20th century.[165]

Toward the middle if the 20th century, remains of a Gothic church were discovered on Olon-sume, present Wuyuan district, in Inner Mongolia, which is considered the church built by Montecorvino with the help of King George of Wongkubu around 1305.[166]

In 1937, a French Franciscan, Louis Gautie wrote in the *Echo de La mission de Chefoo* about the village of Liu-chia-chai (Liujiazhai):

"Liu-chia-chai in 1907 had 114 baptized Christians and 5 catechumens. In the second year of the Emperor Yongle (Ming Dynasty 1405) a Christian family had come from Yu-she-hsien (Shanxi) and founded this Christian community. This Christian community, then, has been in existence for more than 500 years."

Wencelaus Ronflet, another French Franciscan, who worked in the Prefecture of Idu, Shandong, confirmed the information:

"The oldest Christian community of the Prefecture is that of Liu-chia-chai in Pohsing. It should be dated from the 15th century. A funeral stele which was erected in that village in 1387 states that the Liu family came from Nanking. One of the emperors of the Ming Dynasty had taken a daughter of these Liu's clan as a concubine. They lived on imperial estates in Tai-yuan-fu in Shanxi, and emigrated in 1404 to Po-hsing where they founded the village of Liu-chia-chai."[167]

---

[165] Henri Bernard, *Aux Portes de la Chine, Les Missionaires du XVI Siecle, 1514-1588* (Tientsin, Haute Etudes, 1933), p.8.

[166] *China Mission Bulletin*, 1949, no. 4, p. 451.

[167] Id., p. 65.

During the 20th century, discoveries found out the Christian origin of Buddhism monasteries and temples: the two most famous cases are the monastery of Bar Sauma and Mark in Fangshan, south of Beijing and the Da Qin temple, near Louguantai, Zhouzhi, in Shaanxi.

In the second and third decades of the 20th century, the Scheut father Antoon Mostaert (1881-1971), working in the South-East part of the Ordos region, following the discovery of crosses, medals of St. George, found out the Christian origin of the present religion of the Mongol clan of the Erküt, in Ordos region, whose name, according to the father, is the living continuation of the *Yelikewan* of the Yuan Dynasty.[168]

Conclusion

A conclusive evaluation of all these attempts to find the Christian presence in the Chinese world, should, first of all, point out the main reasons of the reduction of the number of Christians during this epoch. Some scholars have already specified:[169]

> *"Although the fall of the Yuan dynasty did not mean the end of Christianity in China, it did impose severe restrictions on the possibilities of active proselytizing by Nestorians and Roman Catholic missionaries. Their main resources of protection and financial support – the Mongol ruling house, the foreign converts whose faith was linked to that of Mongols, and the foreign merchants – were expelled from China, and the commercial routes over land to the Far East were cut off at the end of the 14th century by Tamerlane's conquest of Central Asia. The foreign Nestorian missionaries in all probability left China with the Mongols, since the Metropolitan Province of Khanbaliq had ceased to exist in the beginning of the 16th century, being incorporated in the Metropolitan Province of India. The establishment of a new Chinese dynasty alone, however, does not account for the end of the Roman Catholic missions to China. Other reasons for the decline of those missions not only in China but in the East in general are related to the Order of the Friar Minor*

---

[168] H. Bernard, *La Decouverte de Nestoriens Mongols…*, o.c., pp. 65-74.

[169] Nicolas Standaert (ed.), *Handbook of Christianity in China* (Brill, Leiden, Boston, Koln, 2001), p. 97:

itself, which had become internally divided and suffered heavily from the black plague in 1348, and to the Papacy whose incentives to send missionaries to the East dissipated. With the overall decline of the Mongol Khanates, there was no hope for recovering the Holy Land by means of a Western-Mongol alliance…"

Consequently, we can understand also the reason of the fact that the European missionaries of the 16th century completely ignored the previous attempts done to spread the Christian faith in the Central and Eastern Asia. It was also due to the isolation policy of the Ming China, combined with tragedies, which afflicted western countries. However, the efforts of the missionaries to search for the 'lost Christians' have been indeed admirable.